Conversations with Pinter

Mel Gussow is a longtime drama critic for the New York Times and a winner of the George Jean Nathan Award for Dramatic Criticism, the only drama critic ever to win that prestigious award for reviews published in the Times.

He has written Profiles for the New Yorker on Athol Fugard, Bill Irwin, Peggy Ramsay and Michael Gambon. In addition he has done Profiles for the New York Times Magazine about Tom Stoppard, V.S. Naipaul, Dustin Hoffman, Marsha Norman and Alan Ayckbourn among many others.

Before joining the Times, he was a critic and cultural writer for Newsweek Magazine. The author of *Darryl F. Zanuck: a Biography*, he has taught film at New York University. He was the recipient of a Guggenheim Fellowship and for three years served as the president of the New York Drama Critics Circle. A graduate of Middlebury Colege, he holds a master's degree in journalism from Columbia University.

Mel Gussow

Conversations with Pinter

Nick Hern Books
London

A Nick Hern Book

Conversations with Pinter first published in
Great Britain in 1994 by Nick Hern Books Ltd,
14 Larden Road, London W3 7ST

Copyright © 1994 Mel Gussow

A CIP catalogue record for this book is available
from the British Library

Typeset by Country Setting, Woodchurch,
Kent, TN26 3 TB, and printed in Great Britain by
Biddles Ltd, Guildford and King's Lynn

ISBN 1-85459-201-7 (hardback)
ISBN 1-85459-206-8 (paperback)

Mel Gussow has asserted his right to be identified as the
author of this work

Contents

For my wife, Ann

Introduction

At the end of *The Birthday Party*, as McCann and Goldberg are taking Stanley away to what they euphemistically describe as 'a long convalescence,' the landlady's husband cries out, 'Stan, don't let them tell you what to do!' In conversation in 1988, Harold Pinter said that he lived that line all his life. That stubborn individuality has been a chief motivating factor for the playwright, whether he was rejecting his call up for national service as a young man, or, later in his life, reacting to censors, dismissive critics or nations undermining human rights. In the broadest sense, Pinter has always been a conscientious objector, even as people keep trying to tell him what to do.

Because he has gone his own way, his public image has been that of someone unapproachable. As is often the case, the reality does not equal the perception. Certainly, Pinter is demanding, and he has a reserve with strangers and with those who seek to explicate his work. In our first meeting (in 1971), he was cautious about not entrapping himself in his own words, but he turned out to be responsive, ready to talk about any subject that was raised. Pinter talking is not far removed from Pinter writing, which is one reason the dialogue in his plays has such a natural flow. Over a period of more than four hours, the interview grew into a conversation, as he acknowledges at the end of the session. Our subsequent meetings all became conversations.

That first interview appeared in the New York Times Magazine on 5 December, under the title, 'A Conversation

9

[Pause] With Harold Pinter,' and was a precedent-setting piece for Pinter, who had not been interviewed at such length before. The piece was reprinted in part in the programme for *Old Times* on Broadway and in programmes for various revivals. It has often been quoted in other articles and in books about Pinter and has come to be regarded as an authoritative portrait of the playwright at that time. Rereading it 22 years later, I can still feel the sense of discovery, as if the artist were exploring and learning about his creativity while we talked. This proved to be especially valuable considering Pinter's continuing reluctance to analyze his work or to write introductions to his plays.

Over the years, we have met on a number of occasions, both in London and in New York, at his home and at mine, but most often over lunch. I think a relationship has grown between us, an unusual one for a playwright and a critic, though it is a relationship I also shared with Samuel Beckett.

The Caretaker in London and on Broadway brought Pinter the approbation he had been denied with *The Birthday Party*, which had been treated abusively by the London critics, with the notable exception of Harold Hobson. With *The Homecoming*, he was once again embroiled in controversy. Although the play was dismissed by some of the New York reviewers, it went on to win the Tony Award as best new play, a case of this prize being bestowed on the most deserving and provocative play of the season.

From the first, Pinter asserted his identity away from the mainstream, even away from the main experimental stream. Although he emerged as a playwright in the late 1950's, just after John Osborne and Arnold Wesker, he was unaffiliated with any movement. His early efforts were categorized as comedies of menace. But no label sticks. Impossible to pigeonhole, the work became known as Pinteresque. As the plays continued to grow and expand and as the author moved through disparate, self-generating phases, he became England's foremost living dramatist, with only Tom Stoppard and Alan Ayckbourn as close contenders.

On one level, the plays could be called comedies of language. As Peter Hall, who has staged more Pinter than any other director, said in his autobiography, with him 'words are weapons that the characters use to discomfort or destroy each other; and in defence to conceal feelings.' The plays, his latest, *Moonlight*, definitely included, illustrate one of Pinter's favourite Cockney expressions, 'taking the piss,' which means mocking people with apparent deference, so that they do not know they are being mocked.

Ian Smith, a young Oxford don and cricket team-mate of Pinter's and an astute observer of his work, says that all the plays are about 'Englishness as an urban experience of alienation and dislocation, about establishing a personal identity in relation to other people and to language. Everything is focused. It's about performance and economy of gesture.'

In 1989, our conversations became public when we appeared together on stage at the 92nd Street Y in New York. It was interesting to read in Lois Gordon's commentary in The Pinter Review that she felt the questions and answers, 'virtually a script, were perfect.' I take that as a compliment, but there was, of course, no script, simply two people letting a conversation take its course.

All these conversations take their course. In every interview I arrive fully prepared with questions and areas for discussion, but allow the dialogue to unfold. The more specific the question the more illuminating the response, for example, the opening question of the first dialogue, 'Did you see *Odd Man Out*?' This led him directly into a discussion of the 'mistiness of the past.' I regret that Pinter and I did not know each other at the time of the opening of *The Birthday Party* in London, or later when *The Caretaker* and *The Homecoming* certified the originality of his voice, but those events are alluded to in retrospect. The interviews have been edited for clarity and for repetition, but otherwise appear as

11

they happened. Some passages have been restored.

Pinter has changed in some ways while remaining essentially the same. As he has become more of a public figure, he has been more pilloried by certain segments of the British press. At the same time, he has become surer of himself. As he states, he is more comfortable *in* himself and no longer wishes he could *be* someone else. This fact is partly attributable to his long marriage to Antonia Fraser. The private Pinter can deal more easily with his public persona. But he was always confident (misinterpreted in some quarters as arrogance). In answer to the charge about his violent temper, I can only speak from my first-hand experience. In our many meetings, there has been no sign of hostility (except in his verbal reaction to the attacks he suffers in print). He has also been exceedingly generous with his time and interest.

Throughout the interviews, themes are refrained: his un-dogmatic approach to theatre; his concern about setting the record straight; his organic method, or non-method, of writing, how images possess him and give birth to ideas. As a playwright, he is both intuitive and intellectual, and more *intentional* than generally recognized.

It might be suggested that a major change is his increased political awareness and the eagerness with which he takes a stand in support of various causes. But, as one can see, that interest goes back at least as far as *The Birthday Party*. It is just that he has allowed it to play a more significant role in his life and in his work.

I have talked to a number of people about Pinter – Lady Antonia, his directors, actors, friends and fellow playwrights (Simon Gray, Tom Stoppard, Alan Ayckbourn, David Mamet, Edward Albee, Samuel Beckett). All have expressed their admiration along with their amusement. In person as in his plays, Pinter has great wit and an agile command of the uses of language. He can laugh at himself and at the intellectual pretensions others impose on him. Ever since he said his plays were about 'the weasel under the cocktail cabinet,' and found that phrase engraved in scholarly stone, he has been more watchful of his words.

Because he is eager to know how people he trusts feel about his work, he circulates his manuscripts among a select group. When he wrote his three line ode to the cricket star, Len Hutton ('I saw Len Hutton in his prime/ Another time/ another time'), he sent a copy to Simon Gray, then called him to ask if he had received it. 'Yes,' said Gray, 'but I haven't finished reading it yet.' Recently, Pinter faxed me his latest poem, eight lines on God's inability to bless the living. Soon after, he telephoned me from London and asked if I had received the poem. Naturally I answered, 'Yes, but I haven't finished reading it yet.' Followed by transatlantic laughter.

MEL GUSSOW
December 1993

December 1971

'Something to do with the sofa'

Old Times *deals with a reunion of old friends: a middle-aged married couple, Deeley and Kate, and Anna, Kate's roommate of 20 years ago. As they talk and as they challenge one another with memory, the past is refracted. What really did happen 20 years ago, and what is happening on stage? Has Deeley known Anna before and if so, how well? Were Anna and Kate involved in a lesbian relationship? In the absence of explication and verification on the part of the author, the interpretations of others immediately began to layer the play. Pressed, Peter Hall entered the guessing game, while making it clear that it was strictly his own opinion: 'It's not a play about lesbians. Categorically, no. It's a play about sexuality, and the key to the play is the line, "Normal, what's normal?"'*

The playwright came to New York for the opening of Old Times *(in 1971). With Hall, he was working day and sometimes night on the production, shaping up the cast, all new to the play: Robert Shaw, Mary Ure and Rosemary Harris. My meeting with him took place one afternoon at 3 p.m. after rehearsal. We met in his suite at the Hotel Pierre, where he was staying by himself; his wife, Vivien Merchant, was still starring in* Old Times *in London in the pivotal role of Anna, and their 13-year-old son Daniel was in school. During our talk, which went on into the early evening, Pinter got up to eat a*

*sandwich, pour coffee and, later, Scotch on the rocks.
He smoked continually, punctuating the pauses with
exhalations. There were many pauses and silences, as he
measured his words and verbally edited himself in
search of his exact meaning. He spoke clearly with his
deep, resonant actor's voice; his diction was precise,
sometimes clipped. Consequential and emotional
statements were often said softly and hurriedly, as if he
were afraid someone might overhear him. The picture
was of one totally in command of himself.*

I began by saying that I had seen Old Times *in London
and considered that production a perfect realization of
the play. I wondered what work he was doing on it in
New York. He replied that since the actors were
different, the problem was to strike a balance between
giving them the freedom to interpret and retaining the
shape of the London production. He said that the roles
were affected by the actors' own experience. In answer
to my question, he said that 'unconsciously' he had also
used his own experiences in creating the characters.
'It's obviously something I know about,' he said. There
was a long silence. I decided to ask something specific.
In the play, Deeley claims to have first met his wife after
they both saw the film* Odd Man Out.

MG: Did you see *Odd Man Out*?

HP: Yes.

MG: Do you remember the occasion?

HP: I do, as a matter of fact, but it wasn't alone with one
other person in the cinema, and I didn't meet any girl
when I came out, and I didn't marry her, and so on and
so on. But very likely, very possibly, it was a very hot
day when I saw *Odd Man Out*. What interests me a great
deal is the mistiness of the past. There's a section in the
play, where Deeley says to . . . the friend, that they met in

this pub 20 years before. Well, the fact is they might have and they might not. If you were asked to remember, you really cannot be sure of whom you met 20 years before. And in what circumstances.

MG: Anna has a key line in the play: 'There are some things one remembers even though they may never have happened.' Essentially, that's what you're saying....

HP: That's right.

MG: Of course what's going to happen is that, as with *The Homecoming*, people are going to start playing guessing games: Did they meet? Did they sleep together?

HP: I think it's a waste of time.

MG: From your point of view, the literal fact of a meeting or of a sexual relationship doesn't really matter.

HP: No, it doesn't. The fact is it's terribly difficult to define what happened at any time. I think it's terribly difficult to define what happened yesterday. You know that old Catholic thing, the sin in the head? So much is imagined and that imagining is as true as real.

MG: Does the possibility that the meeting might not have taken place make the relationship less meaningful?

HP: No. The fact that they discuss something that he says took place – even if it did not take place – actually seems to me to recreate the time and the moment vividly in the present, so that it is actually taking place before your very eyes – by the words he is using. By the end of this particular section of the play, they are sharing something in the present.

MG: Which may or many not be based on something that did or did not occur in the past?

17

HP: Right. [Pause.]

MG: I suppose that one would say that something similar occurred in the past. He may not have known Anna, but he probably knew somebody like Anna.

HP: No question. And he may indeed have known Anna. All he says really is that he met her at a pub, and bought her a drink, and they went to a party, and he looked up her skirt. Well, there is *no way* of knowing whether that was Anna or not, but it very possibly could have been. I mean, they did live in the same district.

MG: After *The Homecoming*, you said that you 'couldn't any longer stay in the room with this bunch of people who opened doors and came in and went out. *Landscape* and *Silence* [the two short poetic memory plays that were written between *The Homecoming* and *Old Times*] are in a very different form. There isn't any menace at all.' It seems obvious to me that *Old Times* is an extension of what you did in *Landscape* and *Silence*. I wonder if you feel that way.

HP: I feel that. Yes, I feel that, but I'm never able to be in a position myself to discern, to make any kind of judgment on my own work in terms of development or direction. I leave that to others who seem to be only too happy to do so. I can't, because I'm the fellow in the middle of it all. I can, and do, make a number of judgments, my own personal judgments, about my work in terms of its . . . shape and validity. That concerns me. I'm pretty self-critical, but I don't think about themes when I'm writing. But to try to get back to your question about the doors and all that, I was indeed aware that something else was necessary for me. I couldn't go on with those damn doors. In fact, it's true that in *Old Times* the woman is there, but not there, which pleased me when I managed to do that, when that came through to me.

18

MG: Had you thought about her not being there physically?

HP: Yes. I thought, is she actually going to walk in the door? And if she walked in the door, they would all have to have dinner, because they talk about it over and over. Or is it going to be a question of one of those blackouts? Suddenly there she is – Scene Two! And then I don't know how it happened. I thought, she's there, she's there. I have a note on my first manuscript, on the side of the page: 'Anna there all the time, question mark.' And of course that was it. I was terribly excited when I discovered that.

MG: People are always trying to give literal explanations of your plays. But *Landscape* and *Silence* certainly aren't realistic, and *Old Times* isn't either. Is this a leaving behind of what you consider to be realism? It isn't every man's realism. Do you feel a certain freedom in that regard?

HP: Oh, yes. I did feel a certain freedom in writing *Old Times*.

MG: In comparison with a play like *Tea Party*, in which it is very clear exactly what is happening, there are those blackouts, and then the next scene comes on.

HP: I think the territory has changed a bit for me. One thing that has always *vaguely* interested me – I wouldn't put it very much more than that – is that over the past 13 years, since I started writing plays, so many people have found my characters horrible or inexplicable. Unrecognizable. I have noticed that I've been charged quite often with coldness, even malice, toward my characters. [Pause.]

MG: You don't feel there is any truth to that charge, do you?

19

HP: No, I can't. I've always been concerned with trying to see them as clearly as possible, and without a kind of falsity which is sentimentality. And I still am concerned with that. It's so easy to sentimentalize yourself and characters and every damn thing really. But I've been a little tough, sometimes, with the characters. And I feel now that I possibly have the capacity within me to, I hope, remain rigorous and unsentimental, true to what is actually taking place in these people, *but* not quite so tough. I'll give you an example. In *Tea Party*, which you mentioned, the central character, Disson, has such a terrible time of it. I've set him up to knock him down. He's destroyed from the beginning. I don't like the play for that reason. He's a marked man as soon as he steps on stage.

MG: You haven't created any characters that you would consider villainous?

HP: I suppose that Goldberg and McCann in *The Birthday Party* are regarded as an *evil pair*. But I'm very fond of them.

MG: On the other hand, does anything heroic happen in your plays, or is that an invalid word in your work?

HP: Heroic? [Pause.] No, I don't think that applies. I can't think of anything heroic. But I do think that some characters show a great deal of courage, and possess a great deal of stamina in the face of life. Davies, for instance. I suppose all three characters in *The Caretaker*.

MG: Did you mean before that now you are dealing with people who might be considered more sympathetic?

HP: No. I don't give a damn what other people think. It's entirely their own business. I'm not writing for other people.

20

MG: But you feel there's a change in your characters.

HP: I feel there's a [laugh] change in the weather. Don't misunderstand me. I stick by most things I've written. I said I have reservations about *Tea Party*. I have all sorts of reservations about everything, actually. Until *Old Times*, *The Homecoming* was for me structurally the most satisfying work I have done.

MG: Do you think *Old Times* is, now?

HP: Yes. There's no waste there. *Landscape* and *Silence* are two very short plays. I don't regard *Silence* as an entirely successful piece of work, but I feel that I had to write it. It was a hell of a release.

MG: Are you more satisfied with *Landscape*?

HP: No, I'm not. Structurally, *Landscape* is not quite right. There's nothing I can do about it. But I was going to say that *Old Times* does possess for me a proper balance. I'm sure that many people will disagree totally after they've seen it. With most of my plays, people respond very very strongly.

MG: Time, to a certain extent, has caught up to you. People who weren't willing to accept the earlier plays now look back on them as classics.

HP: It's funny. As you know, *The Birthday Party* was massacred in London in 1958. It ran one week. Yet there were one or two reviews after *Old Times* saying what a pity I had stopped writing plays like *The Birthday Party* – which was the most universally detested play that London had known for a very long time. *The Caretaker* was an awful flop in Paris. People said, what do you think happened? I said they didn't like it and that's all there is to it. It was revived in Paris last year and a tremendous success. I'm not . . .

21

MG: You don't really care what critics think, do you?

HP: I was just about to say that. I really don't. It's not a question whether they like what you do or not. That doesn't interest me very much but I have occasionally been interested in something that actually has been said and it could be said in both a bad review or a good one.

MG: Can you think of any bad things said about you that interested you?

HP: Yes, I can. One thing I thought was particularly funny. Nigel Dennis in the New York Review of Books said something to the effect that my plays were simply acting exercises – for actors. And they were just good parts [laugh] for actors. And that was it. There was absolutely nothing else. There was no content whatsoever, merely postures of actors being sad or happy or whatever. He was most witty, actually, wonderfully destructive and I was fascinated by it. I thought, can this possibly be anything near the truth? Then I felt that these are not my concerns – in writing. I was not writing to give actors good parts. Also I thought, if that's the case, why were so many people suckers or fools? How do they get moved? Why are they moved – if the whole thing is just rubbish. So I decided there was cause for doubt here, on this hypothesis.

MG: When I hear something like that I wonder how much the critic is going on the writer's own background, in this case taking off from the fact that you act. The truth is that you do write good parts for actors.

HP: I hope so. I'm writing for the stage, for actors to act. But it comes second. The characters are there first. It's a good part for an actor if the character possesses a proper and full life.

MG: How do you choose which of your characters you want to play?

HP: I don't think about it at the time of writing. I always have a yen, in due course. I always wanted a crack at Lenny in *The Homecoming*, which I enjoyed doing very much. I played Goldberg. I was a little young for it then. I played Mick in London for about five weeks. I took over for Alan Bates in the middle of the run. Those are the three I actually played. They're all . . . What are they?

MG: Machinators?

HP: Yes. When I was in rep years ago, I always played the sinister parts. My favourite was an MI5 man, immaculately dressed, with a moustache.

MG: In *Landscape*, *Silence* and *Old Times*, you seem to be dealing more with love. Is that something you're conscious of?

HP: Love?

MG: Romance.

HP: Oh, I see what you mean. You mean romantic love. Well, actually, if you want to know the truth, I thought I was dealing with 'love' in *The Homecoming*.

MG: I knew you were going to say that. But it is different.

HP: Yes, it is different.

MG: I can't quote the last line of *Landscape* but it's a love line.

HP: 'Oh my true love I said.'

23

MG: Going back to what you said about being tired of menace. Will the menacing aspects be less important in future plays?

HP: Oh, yes, absolutely. You must understand however that when I said I· was tired of menace, I was using a word that I didn't coin. I never thought of menace myself. It was called 'comedy of menace' quite a long time ago. I never stuck categories on myself, or on any of us. But if what I understand the word menace to mean is certain elements that I have employed in the past in the shape of a particular play, then I don't think it's worthy of much more exploration. After *The Homecoming* I tried writing – odds and ends – and failed, for some time. I remember one or two of them, writing a couple of pages in which again someone came into a room and *all that*. And it was quite dry, quite dry really. No, I'm not at all interested in 'threatening behaviour' any more although I don't think this makes plays like *The Homecoming* and *The Birthday Party* invalid. But you're always stuck. You're stuck as a writer. I'm stuck in my own tracks, whatever they are – for so long. Forever, just because I think I've managed to get out of one trap doesn't mean that I'm not still in a trap.

MG: You don't think you're in a trap now?

HP: I think I am in a trap, always. I sometimes wish desperately that I could write like someone else, *be* someone else. No one particularly. Just if I could put the pen down on paper and suddenly come out in a totally different way. It would be marvellous to find that I was someone else. I often feel that about waking up with myself in the morning. You're trapped with yourself all your damned life. I just get bored with myself and have enough of myself so often. The air around me is always the air I create by moving. If I was someone else I would probably create a different air. I must admit that I also

24

tend to get quite exhausted about being this Harold Pinter fellow. This is quite apart from being me. Harold Pinter sits on my damn back.

MG: Who's Harold Pinter?

HP: He's not me. He's someone else's creation. It's very curious. Quite often when people shake me warmly by the hand and say they're pleased to meet me, I have very mixed feelings – because I'm not quite sure who it is they think they're meeting. In fact, who they are meeting at all. I can't explain it very well. I sometimes feel in others an awful kind of respect which distresses me.

MG: That must be off-putting.

HP: Yes, it is.

MG: What do they expect? A proper phrase or a certain kind of appearance?

HP: Most of them expect me to be a cripple, of course.

MG: A psychological cripple?

HP: No, a physical cripple [laugh].

MG: With a twisted mind?

HP: Some people are very surprised. The fact that one of my main obsessions in life is the game of cricket – I play and watch and read about it all the time – that *apparently* surprises people. It's a normal, healthy activity. I think I'm making a little bit of a meal of all this really. Life is quite tolerable. I have three main interests, I suppose. I live with my family very, very closely. A pretty tight life we have, which is very good. And, of course, I enjoy very much working in the theatre, and in films for that matter. And then cricket.

MG: Is that an equal third?

HP: Oh, yes. An equal third.

MG: Is there any order of precedence?

HP: Well, I don't think I'd ever be at all happy if I were parted from my family. In fact, this little trip is the longest I've been away from them for a very long time. For example, I could never direct a play again in New York because I'd have to be here, and I don't like being away from home too long.

MG: Unless your wife is in the play and you bring your son here.

HP: No, it's too late. We did that with *The Caretaker*, but he's nearly 14 and he's at school. He couldn't possibly leave London.

MG: Is there a fourth part of your life, a lower fourth?

HP: [Pause.] I'm a drinker. I like to drink Scotch and wine, etc., etc., etc. And I'm surely not uncommon, by no means a rare example of the human race, when I say that I like sex and I like thinking about sex, too.

MG: Could you trace the genesis of *Old Times*?

HP: I think I wrote it last winter. Yes, last winter. About a year ago. Well, there's nothing I can tell you about that because it was just a very odd thing really. It was one of those times when you think you're never going to write again. I was lying on the sofa [downstairs in his house in Regent's Park, London] reading the paper and something flashed in my mind. It wasn't anything to do with the paper.

MG: Something to do with the sofa?

HP: The sofa perhaps, but certainly not the paper. I rushed upstairs to my room. I live in a very tall house. I usually find some difficulty getting to the top. But, like lightning, I was up.

MG: What was the thought?

HP: I think it was the first couple of lines in the play. I don't know if they were actually the *first* lines. Two people talking about someone else. But then I really went at it. Incidentally, you did ask me for my 'fourth.' Actually what it is is reading. I read a great deal of poetry.

MG: What poets?

HP: Recently I rediscovered Pope. I haven't read him since school. Lines and verses are always on my mind. Donne. Gerard Manley Hopkins. 'Margaret/ Are you grieving/ over Goldengrove/ unleaving.' Modern poetry. Philip Larkin. Yeats and Eliot.

MG: Do you still write poetry?

HP: Yes. I've written two poems in the last couple of years. Very short. I wrote one about six months ago, about seven lines, but I remember I did 13 drafts of it.

MG: How many drafts of plays do you usually write?

HP: About three. But that was as important to me as anything of mine – that poem. But any poem is – emotionally. I used to write a great deal of poetry a long time ago.

MG: It does seem to me, again about the last three plays, that they're more lyrical. Is that something you're aware of?

HP: Yes, I am aware of it. I think it's very dangerous territory.

MG: Why is it dangerous territory?

HP: You can fall on your arse very easily in attempting to express in, if you like, 'lyrical' terms what is actually happening to people. You can over . . . I did it, in *Silence*, but I cut it. I had a passage. It was very very interesting, actually. When I wrote it, I sent the play, as I always do, to Samuel Beckett, whose opinion, to put it mildly, I respect. And . . . I know him.

MG: Do you always send him your plays?

HP: I began, I think, with *The Homecoming*. Yes, I do always. And he writes the most *suc-cinct* observations. He liked *Silence* very much. He wrote, I remember, one very short remark, something to the effect, 'Suggest you examine or reconsider speech, fourth speech, page five.' [Laugh.] Or whatever it was. So I looked at this speech immediately, and thought, well, I don't see anything wrong with *that*. What do I have to reconsider? It seems to me perfectly in order. But I'll keep it in mind. I will *bear* this matter in mind. I wrote to him and said, thank you, but about this speech I'll listen to it in rehearsals and see what I think of it. Rehearsals started and I heard it, and I thought it was perfectly all right. Then, after about two weeks' rehearsal, Peter Hall came to me – I hadn't been around for a few days – and said, 'There's one speech in this play that I do not think is working at all.' And that was that speech. Off I went and heard it properly again and realized that, of course, Beckett was totally right.

MG: Why wasn't it working?

HP: Well, because . . . it simply went over the top in lyricism. The trouble was that it was basically inaccurate and non-specific and, I think, that is the problem trying to use language in this way. It has to be absolutely specific. If it's at all generalized then it's nothing else but indulgence and it's illegitimate. This applies to the use of any kind of language in any kind of context, but particularly the kind of language you were referring to in these latest plays.

MG: Do you feel that you have to guard against emotion?

HP: I don't quite understand you.

MG: Do you not want to get carried away by something you don't control? Something you cannot do with the accuracy you would demand? [Silence.] The idea of lyricism denotes to me a kind of emotion.

HP: What I'm interested in is emotion which is contained, and felt very, very deeply. Jesus, I really don't want to make a categorical statement about this. But, perhaps, it is ultimately inexpressible. Because I think we express our emotions in so many small ways, all over the place – or can't express them in any other way.

MG: This would seem a lesson to be learned from Beckett, who without demonstrating obvious emotion can be quite emotional.

HP: Yes, with such simplicity of means.

MG: I remember years ago when you wrote about how much Beckett meant to you, at the time you were referring to his novels. How do you feel about his plays?

HP: What can I say? [Silence.]

MG: Do you feel at all as pupil to master?

HP: No, not as pupil to master . . . I think he's the most remarkable writer in the world, that's what I feel. I don't feel pupil to master, for a start, because I don't see where I relate to him at all.

MG: Some people think you do, particularly in the last three plays.

HP: Well, let them say . . . this terrible business of categorizing. I don't feel that on just one level alone, apart from anything else. I feel that his achievements, what he's been able to do in his life, in his writing, are so *far* beyond my own that I don't see any kind of comparison at all. I think he's a great writer. And I'm certainly not that in the way I understand the term, and I do understand the term. The term has a very clear meaning to me. I can tell you who I think are great writers very simply. They're so evident. They're obvious.

MG: Name some obvious.

HP: Well, Dostoevski. This is in *my* mind. Joyce, Proust. They haven't got their names for nothing. And Beckett. [Silence.]

MG: It is something to strive for, isn't it?

HP: I don't see it in those terms. I don't have that kind of ambition. I mean you can't strive to be a Great Writer.

MG: You can strive to be better.

HP: Always strive to be better. [Pause.] One curious element I find in what is called 'literary life' which I notice. I must say, particularly in New York – there's an extraordinary competitiveness. But I must say quite honestly it is something I have never felt remotely. I'm just not an ambitious person.

MG: What first set you to writing plays? Was there something specific that kicked off *The Room*, your very first play?

HP: Oh, yes. I know the image. I know what happened. I was at a party in a house and I was taken for some reason or other to be introduced to a man who lived on the top floor, or an upper floor, and went into his room. He was a slender, middle-aged man in bare feet who was walking about the room. Very sociable and pleasant, and he was making bacon and eggs for an enormous man who was sitting at the table, who was totally silent. And he made his bacon and eggs, and cut bread, and poured tea and gave it to this fellow who was reading a comic. And in the meantime he was talking to us – very, very quickly and lightly. We only had about five minutes but something like that remained. I told a friend I'd like to write a play, there's some play here. And then it all happened. I used to write a great deal of prose in the past, when I was young. And a lot of it, including a novel [*The Dwarfs*] was in dialogue.

MG: To go back for a minute, what did Beckett say about *Old Times*?'

HP: Well, he was . . . very much in favour of it. He did have one reservation, one speech. No, I'm not going to tell which one it was.

MG: Is it still in?

HP: It's in.

MG: Same reason?

HP: No, not the same reason. But I stuck with it. I've no alternative except to stick with it.

MG: Peter Hall didn't spot it?

HP: No. Mind you, it hasn't been an easy one. I must confess that.

MG: Does Beckett send you his plays?

HP: He isn't writing any. He sends me his books, but I never – I'm not in the same position at all. In other words, I don't send him back my notes. I'm very happy to have his. I wouldn't dream of it. Anyway, I have no notes, no notes at all.

MG: When did you first meet Beckett?

HP: From about the age of 19 I started to read him, the novels, and I was quite bowled over by those novels. When we did *The Caretaker* in Paris in 1961, Roger Blin was in it, and one day he said, 'Would you like to meet Beckett?' It was almost too much for me – the thought of such a thing. I had written to him. Eventually. You can imagine. It was 1949 when I started to read Beckett and I didn't manage to write to him until about 1959 – when I wrote him just a short note trying to say what I – something. And got an extremely nice letter back. So then I was in a position of meeting him. The longshot of it is I came into this hotel and he was very vigorous and chatty and extremely affable and extremely friendly and we spent the whole *night* together. And that was really . . . very good. And since then, we've really seen quite a lot of one another.

MG: How do you feel about other playwrights?

HP: Well, my taste is quite catholic. I do enjoy a great deal of writers. I think . . . Edward Bond is a very good writer . . . I've always liked Edward Albee's work. I like Heathcote Williams. When you ask me that kind of question, there are people I could tell you but they suddenly slip my mind.

MG: What about David Storey?

HP: Yes, I think he's a very good writer. I very much like *The Contractor*. It works wonderfully on stage.

MG: If you can put that tent up . . .

HP: They put it up in London all right.

MG: You never have any problems with props.

HP: I don't have any tents, anything like that. But there are problems with coffee cups. You'd be surprised the problems you can run into with coffee cups.

MG: In the manuscript of *Old Times*, there was one page changed. It was all about coffee cups. The change was not of dialogue, but coffee cups and, I think, brandy glasses.

HP: Absolutely, yes.

MG: What happened?

HP: Well, there was one other change in that. I wrote one new line in rehearsal. It was the one addition before London. The line is: 'Yes, I remember.' And that affected all the brandy and the coffee. It came in the middle of brandy and the coffee and affected the whole structure. In this play, the lifting of a coffee cup at the wrong moment can damage the next five minutes. As for the *sipping* of coffee, that can ruin the act. That change was in London. There was no change in the text here at all . . . I did change a silence to a pause. It was a rewrite. This silence was a pretty long silence. Now it's a short pause.

MG: Do you ever rewrite your plays?

33

HP: No. In *The Homecoming* in the first production I did cut some of the section about the cheese roll. In Boston, Elliot Norton, whom I respect as a critic, liked the first act of *The Homecoming* very much and didn't like the second act very much. Someone actually said to me, 'What are you going to do about the second act? Elliot Norton didn't like it.' I said, 'I'm not going to do anything about the second act. The second act is the second act.'

MG: Could you talk about your relationship with Peter Hall?

HP: One or two of my earlier experiences in the theatre with directors were very difficult, really quite impossible. I found the directors very defensive, so that my presence in the theatre was an embarrassment to them. I almost had to ask permission to be allowed to speak. I found myself in the even worse position of having to go round to meet the actors secretly and talk to them. When I first worked with Peter, for a start he invited me to co-direct. That was *The Collection*. He established immediately an atmosphere of total candour, frankness, on all parts. He is entirely lacking in any kind of defensiveness or insecurity in his job. Therefore he allows all the people working with him – the actors, and certainly the author – to say whatever they like, to contribute anything, and to disagree with him openly. He's never upset at being proved wrong. Nor am I, for that matter. This atmosphere which *he* engenders is crucially important for a proper working activity in the theatre.

MG: Does this ever approach anarchy?

HP: Never, because it's his production. He's the final arbiter, although he would equally say it's my play and I'm the final arbiter. We both arrive independently at exactly the same decisions. We have a kind of

communication in which half of it need not be said at all.
I trust his judgment.

MG: What sort of questions would he have for the
playwright?

HP: If he's unclear about any of my intentions, he
simply asks me and I try to tell him what they were. If
there's any confusion . . .

MG: Was there any confusion?

HP: Oh, yes. Undoubtedly the play [*Old Times*] is very
closely grained, tightly grained. There can be no
misunderstandings with the actors and the director. It's a
question of who's feeling what at what time. I must
confess that I am unable to write very explicit stage
directions in the old sense. I find these words impossible
to use – the words you see in brackets. Only very
occasionally do I find it obligatory to do that. So there is
room for misunderstanding.

MG: The only stage direction I can think of offhand is
'he cries.'

HP: Christ, yes.

MG: Silences and pauses count as stage directions.

HP: I'm not talking about that.

MG: You mean (aggrieved) or (humorously)?

HP: Yes, that's right. I think I've done that about two or
three times in this play.

MG: You're very clear about the difference between the
pause and the silence. The silence is the end of a
movement?

HP: Oh, no. These pauses and silences! I've been appalled. Occasionally when I've run into groups of actors, normally abroad, they say a silence is obviously longer than a pause. Right. O.K., so it is. They'll say, this is a pause, so we'll stop. And after the pause we'll start again. I'm sure this happens all over the place and thank goodness I don't know anything about it. From my point of view, these are not in any sense a formal kind of arrangement. The pause is a pause because of what has just happened in the minds and guts of the characters. They spring out of the text. They're not formal conveniences or stresses but part of the body of the action. I'm simply suggesting that if they play it properly they will find that a pause – or whatever the hell it is – is inevitable. And a silence equally means that something has happened to create the impossibility of anyone speaking for a certain amount of time – until they can recover from whatever happened before the silence.

MG: In a sense they stand in for dialogue.

HP: Yes. This is part of the life of the thing. And that's why it's quite distressing to find actors stopping just because it says 'pause.' I always feel that essentially there is a . . . cause.

MG: What are you working on now?

HP: Unfortunately, I'm not in a position to tell you. It is very, very likely that I'm going to enter into a film which is going to be the most difficult task I've ever had in my life – and one which is almost impossible. I'm pretty frightened, but I'm also excited. The thing is, it isn't absolutely concrete.

MG: Would you be interested in directing a film?

HP: Yes, I would. I've written one film script which I

want to direct. But I can't get the money for it, not with the kind of artistic freedom I want. It's an adaptation of a novel by Aidan Higgins, called *Langrishe, Go Down*. It's a curious title. It's on a subject which doesn't seem to be very appealing. It's about three middle-aged spinsters living in a house in Ireland in the 1930's. At the lodge gate there's a cottage and a German philosophy student in his 30's working on a thesis. Now they don't seem to feel this is the brightest subject. [Laugh.]

MG: Of course if you let them name three leading actresses – Vanessa Redgrave, Jane Fonda . . .

HP: Exactly. You hit the nail right on the head. That's the kind of freedom I'm talking about.

MG: How have you chosen your films? Or have they chosen you?

HP: They've been proposed to me.

MG: Not a case of you sitting down and reading *The Servant* or *Accident* or *The Go-Between*, and saying I simply must do this?

HP: It's always been Joe Losey who's given me the books to read. But of course I have been asked to do many other things and declined. These are quite rare items. I've chosen them because I thought something sparked.

MG: Do films act as a chance to get away from a certain part of yourself? The atmospheres are different than in your plays?

HP: I think you may be right. It never occurred to me, actually.

MG: *Accident* and *The Go-Between* deal with time, as do your last three plays. Is there a correlation? Is the past much more of an artistic concern?

HP: Oh, yes, it is. I think I'm more conscious of a kind of ever-present quality in life.

MG: Is it your age?

HP: It may be. It may be. I certainly feel more and more that the past is not past, that it never was past. It's present.

MG: What's future?

HP: I know the future is simply going to be the same thing. It'll never end. You carry all the states with you until the end.

MG: You're always the sum of your previous parts?

HP: But those previous parts are alive and present. The only time I can ever be said to live in the present is when I'm engaged in some physical activity. Really do forget.

MG: Like cricket?

HP: Yes, or squash, for instance. The concentration on the present seems to be absolutely total.

MG: You don't think about past cricket matches?

HP: Not when I'm absolutely engaged.

MG: You don't feel that when you're writing a play?

HP: No. When I'm writing a play I don't know what's coming in. It's coming from somewhere. It isn't the present moment alone, by any means. What it all comes down to is time – your original question. The whole question of time and all its reverberations and possible meanings really does seem to absorb me more and more.

MG: Do you find yourself thinking about your childhood?

HP: No. I seem to have forgotten almost everything about it. If you ask me to tell my childhood stories, I would find it almost impossible. The same thing applies to adolescence. That's slightly different because one remembers kinds of moods, atmospheres, general states, like grief and happiness and things like that. But it's very difficult to be more specific. For example, referring in a way to *Old Times*, if you were to ask me which girl I knew 20 years ago in the month of August, I couldn't say. I knew a number of girls over a certain period and I really couldn't tell you which one. Dates are impossible. Not only couldn't I tell you which girl it was, but I would also not be able to describe what happened between us. One or two images remain. An image of rain, for example, in the street. Or a mirror. I can't remember so much, but it is not actually forgotten. It exists – because it has not simply gone. I carry it with me. If you really remembered everything you would blow up. You can't carry the burden. We discard, surely, so much. We have to.

MG: You haven't written about your adolescence, have you – except in your novel?

HP: Oh, yes, that was terribly about that. No, I don't think I have. All that grief and anguish when you're an adolescent. What the hell was it all about? What caused it, specifically? I don't know. Perhaps it's all too painful. Anyway I don't write about myself.

MG: You aren't interested in politics, are you?

HP: It depends what you mean. I'm very conscious of what's happening in the world. I'm not by any means blind or deaf to the world around me.

MG: I remember your statement about the Vietnam war several years ago.

HP: I think I said the Americans should not have gone in, but they did. They should get out, but they won't. I thought that was too glib myself, a little too rhythmical. But I'm right up to the minute. I read the papers. I have very strong objections to all sorts of things – South Africa, for instance. I'm a member of the anti-apartheid organization. I'm quite horrified by South Africa. Vietnam goes without saying. I think really there is good cause for despair, on the general front . . . We're led to believe that in China there exists a kind of purity and a kind of social solidarity and unity that most countries simply don't possess. The other day, the Chinese representative to the U.N. said something about the great friendship between the Chinese people and the American people. I thought, Jesus Christ, is he also going to commit himself to such totally meaningless, hypocritical expressions? This is a kind of language which politicians share. I don't understand how anyone could be convinced by any statement that issues forth from politicians. It's obviously such rubbish.

MG: You don't let contemporary politics get into your plays?

HP: No, no. Politicians just don't interest me. What, if you like, interests me, is the suffering for which they are responsible. It doesn't interest me – it horrifies me! [Pause.] I mean, Jesus Christ. Well, you know, there's so much. What can one say? It's all so evident.

MG: You don't like to be interviewed, do you?

HP: No, I don't really . . .

MG: You like to talk though, don't you?

HP: Well, if there's someone intelligent to talk to. Otherwise, no. The trouble is that things that are said and are put down in print really stare you in the face for the rest of your life. So much surely depends on how you feel on a particular day. I might say something totally different tomorrow. I don't think anything should be held against me. [Laugh.]

MG: For instance, the weasel under the cocktail cabinet?

HP: Yes, that and some other things. Everyone says things that are absolutely ridiculous, half the time, including myself. They are just not thought out properly. There are some times when one can actually just about think clearly. I mean at the moment I'm working very hard. Oddly enough I've enjoyed our conversation, but I don't know why – because when I came in I was in a very edgy state. You know I came in just two minutes before you and I hadn't eaten, and it was a late night last night, and an early morning. And we had a lot to do today.

MG: I would think that not only in interviews but in conversation, because you are who you are, that people would expect you to say things that would be memorable. That must be a strait jacket.

HP: Absolutely. I don't see any good reason why whatever I say is going to be the least bit interesting. It's this whole problem again of assuming that because you're a writer you're some kind of prophet. Which I certainly am not.

MG: Theory is something you find very antagonistic.

41

HP: Most definitely. For example 'theories of drama' and that kind of thing I find quite unreadable.

MG: You never write introductions to your plays.

HP: A play has to speak for itself. I have written letters to directors – very concrete, I think, not theoretical. About how-to-do, particularly when I can't be there. But I was *extremely* angry when I wrote a letter to a very nice German director, an elderly man called Schweikart, who was doing *Landscape* and *Silence* in Hamburg. I wrote him a letter about the plays, which I hoped would be helpful. And eventually the programme reached me and there was my private letter, printed in the programme. He didn't do it, but the theatre got the letter from him and damn well printed it. It's not public, that business. I was talking, practically, to my director.

MG: Do you think it hurt the appreciation or the understanding of the play to have that in the programme?

HP: No, it probably helped. But that wasn't the point. And equally I'm not interested in helping people to understand it.

MG: But communication is very important to you. You want people to be moved by the work.

HP: But that can only come through the work itself. If it's going to move them, it's going to move them. It's entirely their own responsibility. Naturally I'm very happy when the plays actually do communicate, when the audience enjoys them or finds them recognizable. It is naturally gratifying. But if they don't, they simply don't. And it's not my business to try to encourage them. [Pause.] I have very mixed feelings about audiences. I love some of them. Unfortunately, I did develop as an actor a hostility towards audiences. It may sound childish, but I tend to regard the audience as my enemy.

In other words, they're guilty until they're proved innocent. What is required is simply an act of concentration and they so rarely seem disposed to give it. Half the time, I wonder what the hell, why do they bother to go to the theatre. I'm not at all convinced that the main bulk of a given audience is really interested in the theatre. But when I'm in the audience I have great sympathy with the audience for having to submit to the terrible things on stage. Sometimes I feel dreadfully with them in our mutual suffering.

MG: Do you walk out on many plays?

HP: I walk out a great deal, I'm afraid. But sometimes I stay. I do feel there's no point in wasting time – if you're not with it, if it just isn't up your street, or you'd better be doing something else, like having a drink next door. That doesn't mean the thing you're walking out on is . . . bad. The people who are enjoying it – enjoy it.

MG: When you write plays, do you want a shred of mystery always to exist? Is that part of the fun – to keep secrets?

HP: No. I honestly do not wilfully keep a secret. I can simply only write the play the way I can write. There's no other way I can approach it.

MG: People do like to find enigmas even if they don't exist. I can see with *Old Times* people will say, did it happen or didn't it happen?

HP: I'll tell you one thing about *Old Times*. It happens. It all happens. [Silence.]

MG: How do you feel about directors' theatre, in which the director much more than the playwright has his imprint on the dramatic work? Does that offend you as a playwright? Does a play need a playwright?

HP: All I can say is my own taste. My inclination is to say, yes, a play does need a playwright. I mean, I'm a fairly traditional person. What interests me in the theatre is, firstly, a play written by one writer, and of course done to a degree of excellence. As a director myself I appreciate that. Group theatre that I've seen, creation by a group, very, very rarely interests me – I do admire a certain company in England, called The Freehold, and the Open Theater here.

But what I abhor really is the climbing over the audience kind of display and the one great belch from a group of squirming people. I find it extremely tedious – and uninformative. Why don't they just do it by themselves? I just find these a kind of display, exhibition, masquerading under a guise of togetherness, of attempting a 'major statement' – which I never believe in, and think is always a gross generalization.

MG: Any major statement?

HP: I think *any* major statement, too, certainly, but particularly major statements in that kind of context. 'Understand the love which you are capable' and 'come to me and I'll come to you' or 'hit me and I'll hit you.' This is a free-for-all of *naive* and totally meaningless generalizations. I think the actors in so many of these cases are under a severe delusion that they themselves as people have something to offer others, that they can teach, that they can inform other people, that they are in a position to help or illuminate which I think is a very dubious posture.

MG: Because they are actors?

HP: No, because nobody is in that position. And nobody is entitled to consider himself in such a position. I certainly don't myself. There is clearly a kind of arrogance involved in that attitude . . . I've just been directing a play by James Joyce, *Exiles*. And for all of us doing it, trying to find precisely what the mind writing the play is about, to locate precisely what is taking place in this one mind, is most exciting.

MG: What's in your future?

HP: I don't know what I'll do. I have no idea what's to come, really. I've always been left with this empty space in front of me after finishing a play. And it gets longer and longer.

MG: After *The Homecoming* did you feel you wouldn't write a play again?

HP: Yes. I certainly did. Very, very depressing.

MG: What did you do?

HP: I kept busy I suppose, one way or the other. Films, I suppose. It's not quite the same thing as something really coming out from the bottom of your spine. Words anyway become more difficult all the time, the older you get. What else can one possibly write? Something seems to happen. I feel quite cheerful about the prospect in front of me.

MG: You have said that after finishing a play you feel like wringing its neck for one last time. Have you ever thought of going back to an old play of yours and wringing its neck one last time?

HP: The only time I've ever done anything remotely like that was in *The Birthday Party*. When I did it myself at the Aldwych in 1964, in rehearsal I made a pretty strong cut in act three. Coming back to it after six years I really felt that it needed it, that it was wrong in the first place. But in the main I can't go back because I've got to leave it. Leave it. I have such mixed feelings about my previous work. Sometimes I feel absolutely sick of all the plays I've written. I can't bear to look at them or think about them or hear about them. They're a very strange burden. But quite on the other hand, and almost equally strongly occasionally – not very often – I pick up one or two of them and think – that's not bad! Quite enjoy them, and pleased that I've actually written them. But the really odd thing is that I've written probably 15 plays, including short plays obviously, and I really don't know how I've done it. I don't know where they come from and how I managed to write any of them at all. I really don't. It's most odd. I can't think how I did all that work.

MG: If you don't know, who would know?

HP: My wife, probably, could remember more than I.

MG: How long did it take for the first draft of *Old Times*?

HP: About three days.

MG: The second draft?

HP: That took a few months.

MG: When you finished, did you have the play read to you?

HP: I read the play aloud to myself, so I know if it's playable. I walk the characters through. I move them about. I play all the parts.

MG: Does anybody watch?

HP: I'm also the audience.

MG: Do you laugh?

HP: I laugh during the writing, sometimes.

MG: Does the title come first?

HP: No.

MG: Last?

HP: Yes.

MG: Any working title while you were writing?

HP: There was, yes. A silly one. In the play Anna talks about the cafes we found where artists and writers and sometimes actors collected, and 'others with dancers.' And I couldn't get the phrase 'and others with dancers' out of my mind. I did actually put 'Others with Dancers,' and thought, no, no, that's not it at all. No, I was very pleased about the title when it eventually came. It did strike me as accurate.

MG: I think it really sums it up. Actually all your titles have been very apt.

HP: Well, thanks. It's very important for me . . . Incidentally, for . . . interest, do you know which play took the longest time to write? *Silence.*

MG: Why?

HP: Oh, well, the structure was so difficult . . . But there you are. It just did.

MG: It wasn't three days on the first draft?

HP: Oh, God no. [Pause.] I'll have to get ready soon, by the way. We've been here an awfully long time. This is the longest interview I've ever had in my life. Well, actually, let's face it, it has been a conversation.

December 1979

'Two people in a pub . . . talking about the past'

In December 1979, shortly before the Broadway opening of Betrayal, *Pinter and I met, late in the afternoon, in his New York hotel suite. I had seen* Betrayal *the previous July at the National Theatre and felt that in mood and subject it was clearly related to* Old Times *and* No Man's Land. *With that in mind, I asked my first question.*

MG: One could say that your first six full-length plays were two trilogies. The first three deal with a lower-class or lower middle-class situation with a certain raffish behaviour on the part of the characters. In the next three, people work generally in the areas of art, literature and publishing. The first three are comedies of menace, the next three deal in varying degrees with memory, loss of memory, love, the absence of love. *Landscape* and *Silence* could be regarded as transitional plays. Is this anything you're conscious of?

HP: I can't look back over my work and make any kind of judgment on it. I see from what you say that there are certain distinctions to be made between the later plays and earlier plays. But is that not always the case in any writer's work?

MG: Not necessarily. Certainly not in the writer who doesn't grow.

HP: Well, I would say that we all change. [Pause.] Damn it . . . in terms of age . . . when did I write *'The Birthday Party*? I think it was 1957.

MG: When you were in your 20's, and then the next plays when you were in your 30's and the last three when you were in your 40's .

HP: That's right. And now I'm hitting 50. [Laugh.]

MG: Have you changed? Is it a different process you go through when you're writing?

HP: It's exactly the same. What invariably happens is that either an image or a couple of sentences come to me and I go on from there. I always start at the beginning of a play. I've been starting at the beginning for years.

MG: And ending at the end?

HP: And ending at the end.

MG: What was the initial image for *Betrayal*?

HP: Two people at a pub . . . meeting after some time.

MG: A man and a woman?

HP: Yes, yes.

MG: Did you know who they were?

HP: No, truly didn't. Found out. [Pause.] I remember when I wrote *No Man's Land*, I was in a taxi one night coming back from somewhere and suddenly a line, a few words came into mind. I had no pencil. I got back to the house and wrote those lines down. I can't remember exactly what they were, but it was the very beginning of the play, and I didn't know who said them. As you know, I don't proceed from any kind of system or theory.

MG: With *Betrayal* did you actually see two people sitting in a pub or was it just an imagined event?

HP: No. God knows what it was!

MG: When did you decide to go backwards in time instead of forwards as usual?

HP: After I found out what they were talking about. They were talking about the past. So, I thought I'd better go back there and see what happened.

MG: In *Old Times*, you stayed right in the present. You didn't show us what happened. You talked about what might have happened.

HP: In this case, when I realized the implications of the play, I knew there was only one way to go and that was backwards. The actual structure of the play seemed to dictate itself. You have two people in a pub and you wonder when they first met. Where was it? When I realized what was going on, this movement in time, I was very excited by it.

MG: How early did the theme of *Betrayal* arise?

HP: It was evident more or less straight away that there were only going to be three main characters, and that they'd been up to something.

MG: In the play, there are many different types of betrayal. Could you say which is worse?

HP: Certainly not! [Laugh.] Wouldn't dream of making any kind of value judgment.

MG: You start to wonder if the wife didn't betray her lover by having a child by her husband, or by telling her husband about her affair with a lover without telling her lover she was telling her husband.

HP: The men also make certain betrayals. I wouldn't want it all to come down to the lady.

MG: One might say the primary betrayal is with the men because they begin as best friends. And still are friends.

HP: I think so, but it will never quite be the same.

MG: They still meet for their periodic luncheons. They talk about authors and seem to disagree about them all the time. Did you consider bringing the writers in?

HP: I knew from very early on that there were only three characters.

MG: Did you always know their professions?

HP: No. All that clicked in after a while. And as soon as Jerry announced in the first scene that Casey was his author, I found that Robert was his publisher.

MG: There's a phrase that Martin Esslin used about *Betrayal* – the 'fallibility of memory.' In *Old Times*, *No Man's Land* and *Betrayal*, you never know if certain things did or did not take place. The subject of memory seems to interest you more and more. Do you find yourself thinking about your past? Does your work on the screenplay for Proust's *Remembrance of Things Past* bear a responsibility here?

HP: I wrote *Landscape* and *Silence* and *Old Times* before I wrote the Proust screenplay, and it is certainly true that those plays concern themselves with memory and the past. But Proust did open up a hell of a world for me. It was really a great year working on Proust, although the screenplay can never in any way rival the work which it served, and which is an evident masterpiece. I've just done another screenplay, by the way. *The French Lieutenant's Woman.* That's been bloody, bloody hard. It's a remarkable book. The problems involved in transposing it to film are quite considerable. It pretends to be a Victorian novel, but it isn't. It's a modern novel, and it's made clear by the author that he's writing it now. That whole idea had to be retained.

MG: How did you do it? Does the novelist tell the story?

HP: Ah, well, I'm not going to tell you the secret. Karel Reisz [the director] and I just stumbled upon a way of looking at it, which I hope mirrors what the author [John Fowles] does in his original.

MG: Once again, you're dealing with the past, with memory. How is your memory?

HP: I have a strange kind of memory. I think I really look back into a kind of fog most of the time, and things loom out of the fog. Some things I have to force myself to remember. I bring them back by an act of will. It appals me that I've actually forgotten things, which at the time meant a great deal to me.

MG: Do your plays have more to do with your life than we know?

HP: They have more to do with my life than *I* know. [Long pause.] I know the characters to be a part of my life. I didn't know them before, but I know them now. They exist.

MG: But as fictional characters?

HP: Yes. It would be wrong to say that I was writing about things I remembered personally. [Long pause.] I just think it's all happened to all of us.

MG: Did the fact that your marriage [to Vivien Merchant] broke up before you wrote *Betrayal* have any effect on the writing of the play?

HP: I'm very glad you asked me that question, because I can tell you that it's totally irrelevant. One thing has absolutely nothing to do with another.

MG: One reason why people raise the question is that when the play was done at the National Theatre, in the programme you made reference to your present relationship with Lady Antonia Fraser, and people said, 'That's what the play is about . . .'

HP: Well, that's really nonsense. Normally, in programmes, they say he is 'married to so and so'. *I* said *I* was 'living with' Antonia Fraser, which was the case. I simply decided to put the thing very clearly because that's what the situation was. All those rumours and gossip. I thought I might as well put the matter straight in a context, which was actually a tradition of programme notes. But it has absolutely nothing to do with the play.

MG: I notice that the last three plays were dedicated to Peter Hall, Jimmy Wax and Simon Gray. Obviously they're very important people to you. Could you take them one by one and say something about what their effect has been on your writing, on your life?

HP: Jimmy Wax is my agent, and I often refer to him as the Reverend Wax because I believe him to be a very wise man. He's been my agent from the very beginning. We met in an attic in Bristol when I was on tour there with a farce and had just written *The Room*. The person

54

with whom I was staying suggested that I read *The Room* to him, which I did, and we've had a very close association since then. I've been associated with Peter Hall since 1963, when he asked me to go to the Aldwych and we did *The Collection* together there for the Royal Shakespeare Company. I think he does my work with total understanding and authority.

I remember a story about him which never fails to amuse me. I think it's very characteristic of the man. We were on tour with *The Homecoming* in Brighton, and were just about to go into London. Brighton was the last week of quite a long tour. We were going to the theatre to see the actors. I said to him, 'I really think, Peter, that they've had enough notes. I think we should leave them alone, because I can't see how they're going to absorb more notes. Why don't we just let them get on with it and play it for the last few days before we get to London?' He said, 'Yes, I think you're probably right.' We got to the theatre, and he said to the actors, 'I'm not at all sure that I should give you any notes at all this morning, because you've probably had enough. However, I would just make one or two observations.' And we were there for three hours. Note after note after note after note. He was, of course, absolutely right.

As for Simon Gray, to complete that trio, I admire him tremendously. I think he's a writer of *incredible* vividness and vigour and wit. I always have a whale of a time directing his plays.

MG: A whale?

HP: A whale, yes. We're also very close friends.

MG: Do you see any kinship between his work and yours?

HP: I believe that they're quite different. Various attributes he possesses I do not have. His wit. I think I can be quite funny now and again. But he has the ability to bring the house down in the most exhilarating fashion. He can do it with one line. In 'Otherwise Engaged,' when the brother accuses Simon Hench of telling all his clever metropolitan friends that 'my wife and I are imbeciles,' and Simon says, 'I swear to you, Stephen, I've never told a soul' – that's an enormous one line laugh, which I admire tremendously.

MG: What would happen if Simon Hench or Ben Butley wandered into one of your plays?

HP: Are you suggesting that we write a double play?

MG: By directing his work, it almost becomes a double play.

HP: No. When I'm directing his plays, I never propose a line. What we always consider together are cuts, an economizing of the text. His plays are packed. My plays may appear to be extremely long, but in fact they're quite short. [Laugh.] That is a difference in technique. He looks forward to rehearsal to refine his own text.

MG: And yours is already refined before you get to rehearsal?

HP: I believe that's so. Yes.

MG: Do you make any changes during rehearsal?

HP: I did make a few small cuts in *No Man's Land* in rehearsal – and in *The Homecoming*.

MG: Did you make any changes in *Betrayal*?

HP: In rehearsal in London, I did three things. I cut one word, 'please'. I also took out a pause and I inserted a pause.

56

MG: And that made all the difference?

HP: That made all the *damn* difference.

MG: Recently I talked to Beckett in Paris. He said that he really was tired of talking about his work. I felt that he meant that totally, that he just didn't want to talk about it ever again.

HP: Well, I don't get very much pleasure out of talking about my work either. I never know what I could possibly say about it that would be of any real value or interest.

MG: It certainly never pays to try to clear up any mysteries.

HP: I think Beckett himself said years ago that he's writing in the dark, and I understand that. What the hell is there to say?

MG: Shaw found a lot to say.

HP: Oh, Shaw, yes. As you've gathered, I don't find a lot to say.

MG: When you direct your own work, you have to talk to the actors. You have to tell them things about the play.

HP: I'm quite happy to do that, because one is dealing with specific facts in the very concrete act of rehearsal. I'm not at all shy, talking about the characters and what I believe they're doing, when I'm in rehearsal with actors. But I'm not disposed happily to make public statements. We always seem to talk very easily together, but, believe me, I don't find this common. And also I have a certain constraint: that's to do with the question of pretension or self-importance.

MG: If you talked about it, it would lend itself . . .

HP: Well, I am talking about it. The very act of our conversation is that I'm aware that if anything comes out of this . . .

MG: It will be carved in stone?

HP: This is going to be printed . . . I was asked by a friend of mine here to go to Columbia University and talk to a few people. I couldn't do it. I didn't know what the hell I would talk about. I have given two speeches in my life. The last one was a long time ago, about the same time as we last talked. I went to Germany. I received the Shakespeare Prize and to receive the damn thing, I had to make a speech. It wasn't the delivery of the speech that worried me, it was the writing. I find it a terrible sweat. Since we last spoke, I've only given one interview, which was at the time of National Theatre strike when I was directing *Close of Play*. I felt obliged to say something then. But I just prefer getting on with the work.

MG: I saw you on stage at the National last year reading poetry.

HP: Oh, that's different. I enjoy doing that. I like reading poetry aloud, always have. The work of poets I admire. Next autumn I'm going to make a film for television about three poets, George Barker, John Heath-Stubbs and W. S. Graham. They've been writing poetry for the last 50 years, and they're very little known either in England or America. They're not whiz kids, you see. They're all great characters and remarkable poets.

MG: Do you sometimes think you would have liked the life of a poet? Would that have appealed to you more than the life of a playwright?

HP: Yes! [Pause.]

MG: Hard to make a living as a poet.

HP: I'm afraid so. How these particular men have done it, I really don't know. Heath-Stubbs is totally blind. And Graham lives in a little cottage in Cornwall. What they're interested in is language, and they haven't budged. I admire them very much. These people are poets. I'm an occasional poet. That's a very different matter . . . I'm also interested in language. Language is my concern. But it comes out in this form.

MG: Years ago, Kenneth Tynan referred to your 'aimlessly iterated phrases'.

HP: Aimlessly?

MG: 'Aimlessly iterated phrases'.

HP: Well, he's quite entitled to his opinion, but I will say that nothing I've written is 'aimless'. I think every sentence is a nugget. You should be able to hold it in your hand – or whatever you do with a nugget – and say, it exists, it's paying for its keep. It's essential.

MG: You don't waste words.

HP: I try not to waste words.

MG: How long did it take to write *Betrayal*?

HP: It adhered to my normal rhythm, which is about three months. There comes a point when I say to myself, there's nothing more I can do with this damn thing, and that's it.

MG: In our last talk, we spoke about the fact that when you finish a play, you always want to 'wring its neck

59

once more'. Do you ever give it one more turn through the typewriter?

HP: No. It may sound fanciful, but it's to do with the fact that the play then exists, and I have to respect that life. I could do it damage by buggering about with it. But I'm not sure I've ever given full service to anything I've written.

MG: In the case of *Betrayal*, would you have considered writing another scene, going back another few years?

HP: During the course of writing *Betrayal*, I was well aware that I could have branched out in other directions. There were clearly a number of scenes that could be written, that could be given life. But I looked at it very carefully and came to the decision that what was being given was enough, and that to attempt to unearth more would be, in fact, wasteful. It would clog the wheels.

MG: When are your plays over?

HP: You just know. It's so easy to fuck a play up really.

MG: Have you ever?

HP: I have not! I'm not sure that I've ever given full service to anything I've written. That's probably not possible. I don't know of any perfect work. Do you? Recently I saw *Death of a Salesman* in London, which, as always, had the most terrific impact. But I don't think it's perfect. I'm sure Arthur Miller would agree.

MG: Arthur Miller might not agree. He might think it was perfect.

HP: [Laugh.] It's *almost* perfect.

MG: *Waiting for Godot* is perfect. And *Endgame*.

HP: I certainly think *Endgame* is perfect. [Pause.]

MG: Is *Hamlet* perfect?

HP: No, *Hamlet* isn't perfect.

MG: He should have wrung its neck once more?

HP: No, I'm glad he left it alone . . . What does perfection mean? How can it ever be achieved. It doesn't exist, although I've just said that *Endgame* is perfect. [Laugh.]

MG: Speaking of less than perfect, why did you choose to direct *Blithe Spirit*? Do you particularly like Noël Coward?

HP: Well, yes. I can't say that I read very much Coward, but I was asked by Peter Hall to consider the play. I read it and I thought it'd be fun to do. And it wasn't fun to do. It was very very hard to do.

MG: Do you feel any affinity with Coward?

HP: I don't feel very much affinity, but I did admire a great deal about Coward. He was a man of considerable range, and, again, he could bring the house down. I love the fun and games of *Blithe Spirit*. But one found that even he, a pretty economical writer, went in for a kind of exposition that was somewhat laboured. There was nothing one could do about it. There was no question of cutting it. You had to live with it. That was the play.

MG: Do you like Coward better than Rattigan?

HP: I acted in a quite a lot of Rattigan, you know, when I was in rep. I think he's a very underestimated writer. They almost killed him. He was, as you know, suddenly shat upon. Very heavily. And by people who have no right to do such a thing.

MG: The London critics were very harsh on *The Rear Column, Close of Play* and *Betrayal,* two of Gray's, one of yours. Is it a matter of expectation, of what they think a playwright should do?

HP: There is a definite and rather amusing resistance on the part of the London critics to a writer doing anything at all different. Apart from *The Caretaker,* which is a hell of a long time ago, I've never really been well received by the critics. The critics don't like play 'C,' but, invariably, when play 'D' arrives, they point immediately to the virtues that play 'C' possessed and regard play 'D' as a deviation. This goes on all the time. A second point is the generation thing. I've been writing for quite a long time, and in England over the last few years, there has been a very, very strong *young* wave of political playwrights. They're admired – in some cases, quite properly. But a number of the critics seem to feel that a man of my age and temperament and disposition is slightly out of kilter with the needs of the time. They're irritated by the fact that I continue to write just exactly what I want to write, but I'm not really much bothered by it. You know, I was brought up in a very hard school. *The Birthday Party* in 1958 ran a week, which is a good way of getting old in this profession. In 1958, *The Birthday Party* was generally found to be incomprehensible. It's now been done throughout the world, and it's clearly *comprehensible.* Some things change. The play hasn't changed. It's exactly the same.

MG: What are you working on now?

HP: A couple of months ago I suddenly found a play I'd written many many years ago, a full-length play, which I put aside at the time. I wrote it after *The Birthday Party* and before *The Caretaker.* I simply put it aside. I didn't discard it. I held on to it. I hadn't thought about it for years. I read it as a stranger over a 20 year distance, and I really laughed quite a lot. In consequence, I'm going to direct it. It's called *The Hothouse*. It takes place in some kind of state-subsidized mental home. It's all about the staff. One never sees the patients, but they're there. It was an odd experience to read it, and I've done a bit of work on it. I've made a few cuts. I noted a certain self-indulgence in the writing.

MG: Is it like your other plays?

HP: I can recognize certain features, certain outpourings of wild bravura, speeches which remind me vaguely of Mick in *The Caretaker*. I want to do the play rather quietly at the Hampstead Theatre Club. I thought I would have a bit of fun.

MG: This will be the first time you've directed an original production of one of your plays.

HP: Yes, it will be. It's simply a different kettle of fish. [Pause.] It was odd reading it. I had extracted one or two short sketches out of it sometime in the sixties. But I would just like to see if I can get the juices out of it.

MG: Are you working on a new play?

HP: No, no, I'm not. No, no. I have a pretty busy year coming in front of me, but that has nothing to do with it. I could still be working on a new play. The answer is I'm not. I seem to write a play every four or five years. I think I will write another play – sometime.

December 1988

'Stan, don't let them tell you what to do'

For many years, Pinter paralleled in his personal life the enigmatic quality of his plays. In the 1980's, however, his political position became more widely known. Through PEN and Amnesty International, he was an outspoken advocate of human rights and a vigorous opponent of suppression in all countries. In 1988, John Mortimer suggested to Pinter that meetings of anti-Establishmentarians should be convened to express their mounting dissatisfaction with Margaret Thatcher. Because of the date of the first meeting, the colloquy came to be known as the 20th June Group. Besides the Pinters and the Mortimers, among those who participated were David Hare, Margaret Drabble, Michael Holroyd, Germaine Greer, Ian McEwan, Angela Carter and Salman Rushdie. The meetings remained casual, serious and private, with people invited to deliver addresses on such subjects as censorship and civil liberties.

At the same time, the politicization of Pinter was making itself more evident in his art. His last two plays, One for the Road and Mountain Language, were brief works about political persecution and incarceration. He had also written three screenplays with political content: adaptations of Fred Uhlman's Reunion; Margaret Atwood's The Handmaid's Tale and, for Granada Television, Elizabeth Bowen's The Heat of the Day.

Late in 1988, Pinter visited New York with his wife to spend time with her two youngest children, both of whom were living in the United States, and to confer with Carey Perloff, the artistic director of the CSC Repertory. The CSC was planning an Off Broadway run of The Birthday Party, *which it had revived the previous season. Over lunch, Pinter spoke about the turns in his career and how they reflected his growing dismay about world affairs. Frequently he returned to the subjects of human rights, censorship and United States foreign policy in Central America.*

MG: In one of his journals, Simon Gray characterized *One for the Road* as a 'triumph of evil over innocence,' in other words, he said, it was the opposite of *King Lear.* Does that statement have a validity?

HP: *One for the Road* is short and brutal. *Mountain Language* is even shorter and more brutal. *Mountain Language* is 20 minutes. I directed it at the National Theatre and it's a full-scale production, in terms of design, light, sound, costumes, a full-scale production of a 20 minute play. It begins at 6:15 and it's all over by 6:35. It's on the Lyttelton stage, which is a 900 seat theatre. For a noon performance there were 750 people. It's a hell of a cast: Michael Gambon, Miranda Richardson and Eileen Atkins.

I've also directed it on the BBC and it'll be transmitted in a couple of weeks – to their own surprise because of the government's recent white paper on broadcasting. Television and radio are now on a very tight wavelength. They're being reined in. The whole idea is to deregulate television and be very much more like American television. Those things on television which we took for granted for so many years – the drama, the serious discussions, religious programmes, debates, documentaries – if you come back in ten years' time, it will all be over. It will just be various degrees of rubbish.

It's surprising that *Mountain Language* is being done, because it's a strong and rather unpleasant piece of work. It's really a series of short sharp images inside and outside a prison. The play begins with a group of women waiting to be allowed to enter a prison where their relations are. It becomes clear very quickly that the women have been waiting out there for eight hours. It's very cold and one of them has been bitten by a Doberman pinscher during the course of the day.

A sudden outrage happens in the very first scene. One of the women is threatened sexually. The officer informs the women that they cannot speak their own language, their mountain language. Their language is banned, outlawed. We assumed there's a language they speak, like Welsh or Gaelic, Basque, Estonian or Kurdish, although the play is in English. The old woman is not able to speak any other language. She can't speak the language of the capital, so she can't speak to her son. The other woman finds her husband in a corridor with a hood over his head; she reckons it's her husband because of his clothes. The play ends in a pretty flat and brutal way . . . I've just tried to describe it.

MG: That's a great deal of plot for 20 minutes.

HP: It's action-packed. I haven't yet heard anyone complain that it's only 20 minutes long. The audience seems quite relieved to get out of there, as soon as possible.

MG: As you began writing it, did you know it was going to be a short play?

HP: Actually, I wrote it over a period of three years. I started it three years ago and wrote about four or five pages. I didn't think it was working and I nearly threw it away, except that Antonia read it and insisted that I keep it. Three years later, I picked it up again and suddenly whipped into it, and finished it. I think I always knew it was a pretty short play, but I didn't know how short. I didn't know how it was going to go, when I picked it up again.

There was a certain amount of discussion in England about what the play refers to. It was inspired by my visit to Turkey with Arthur Miller, my experience with the Kurds, who, as you know, are not allowed to speak their own language. It's a criminal offense. It's not a play about the Turks and the Kurds because if you were to write a play about the Turks and the Kurds, it would take longer than 20 minutes, for a start. It would take a great deal of historical research. From my point of view, the play is about suppression of language and the loss of freedom of expression. I feel, therefore, it is as relevant in England as it is in Turkey. A number of Kurds have said that the play touches them and their lives. But I believe it also reflects what's happening in England today – the suppression of ideas, speech and thought.

MG: Would you carry it one step further and say, it also reflects what's happening in America?

HP: I have a lot to say about American foreign policy but I really wouldn't want to set myself up as an authority on American domestic affairs, not having lived here for a very long time. I am certainly aware of a number of aspects of America's internal life, which I find disturbing and bewildering. I think there's a similar attitude in the United States and England about how to treat the poor, the homeless, the disabled, which mainly is to ignore them.

The play has to do with a kind of strangulation. Let me be a little more specific about England. One section of the community in England is being singled out, and that is the homosexual section, singled out for censorship and repression. You've heard about Clause 28? Well, that's it. Clause 28 is quite a pervasive act, a law, which is very very dangerous indeed. The effects can already be seen: books being banned from libraries and plays which cannot be shown in schools, plays which touched upon the gay scene and have been withdrawn under pressure. The Clause precisely refers to the promotion of homosexuality, to say that it is harmless, or normal. And that's against the law. I really think it's reminiscent of the Jews in the 30's in Germany. I believe there is a reference to this suppression in my play. Something that could be described as uncommon or slightly out of the norm is regarded as an alien force, something to be suppressed and disciplined. That was one of the references in my play, but I didn't know that when I wrote it. I have to tell you, I just write, as I always did [snaps his fingers]. I still don't theorize at all – only talking to you now.

MG: In *One for the Road* and *Mountain Language*, at least covertly you are theorizing.

HP: Not really. I don't think that about either play.

MG: It could be said that you've always written political plays, starting with *The Birthday Party*.

HP: I think that's true. *The Dumb Waiter*, too.

MG: *The Birthday Party* has the same story as *One for the Road*?

HP: It's the destruction of an individual, the independent voice of an individual. I believe that is precisely what the United States is doing to Nicaragua. It's a horrifying act. If you see child abuse, you recognize it and you're horrified. If you do it yourself, you apparently don't know what you're doing. In my play, the woman whose hand has been bitten by this Doberman pinscher is asked by an officer, 'Who did this?' She simply stares at him.

She looks frightened; she doesn't know what to say. Naturally he shouts. He bellows: 'Who did this?' It's his thought that she provoked it. This is clearly the case with the U.S. and Nicaragua.

MG: Have you been to Nicaragua?

HP: I have indeed and I am the chairman of the arts for Nicaragua fund in England. We're trying to do our best on all levels to support artists in Nicaragua, even on the level of paintbrushes. When I went there, I took 300 paintbrushes and gave them to Ernesto Cardenal.

MG: Didn't they stop you at Customs and wonder what you were doing with 300 paintbrushes?

HP: The word had gone through that they were on their way. I was, in fact, the guest of the government.

MG: In their book about your work, Guido Almansi and Simon Henderson say, 'He is an author without authority, a communicator in the paradoxical position of having nothing to say.' Later they say, 'He is the maestro of the tittle-tattle of quotidian verbiage.'

HP: The term, 'nothing to say', is a very interesting use of language. It is as if the author is making a speech. The author in fact is writing a play. I've always maintained that the life of any play consists in its dramatic authenticity, if it's true to itself. Something is being said, but the playwright isn't necessarily saying it. It's the play that's saying it . . . It could be said that *One for the Road* and *Mountain Language* are more direct statements than other plays. At the same time, they're both – I repeat – a series of short, sharp, brutal images, which, I hope, amount to a play and not a public statement. Writing such things might be seen as a political act.

MG: What if you wrote *The Birthday Party* today and said it was inspired by your trip to Turkey and by your knowledge of the Kurds?

HP: It so happens it was inspired by two things. I met this fellow in a seaside boarding-house when I was on tour as an actor. He lived in this attic and used to play the piano on the pier. He was a totally lonely man. That's all I knew about him, but his image remained with me for some years. I thought, what would happen if two people knocked on his door? That knock was the second thing. The idea of the knock came from my knowledge of the Gestapo. I'll never forget: it was 1953 or 1954. The war had only been over less than ten years. It was very much on my mind.

I came across a letter I wrote to Peter Wood, the director of *The Birthday Party*. It's absolutely relevant. It was before we had gone into rehearsal and he had asked me to clarify, to put a final message into the play so that everyone would know what it was about. This letter was a letter of refusal to do such things. Between you and me, the play showed how the bastards . . . how religious forces ruin our lives. But who's going to say that in the play? That would be impossible. I said to Peter Wood, did he want Petey, the old man, to act as a chorus? All Petey says is one of the most important lines I've ever written. As Stan is taken away, Petey says, 'Stan, don't let them tell you what to do.' I've lived that line all my damn life. Never more than now.

MG: That's a theme running through the plays. Could you trace it?

HP: Ruth in *The Homecoming* – no one can tell her what to do. She is the nearest to a free woman that I've ever written – a free and independent mind. [Pause.] I understand your interest in me as a playwright. But I'm more interested in myself as a citizen. We still say we live in free countries, but we damn well better be able to speak freely. And it's our responsibility to say precisely what we think.

MG: Could you continue to exist as a citizen without dramatizing what you feel?

HP: Oh, yes. Don't forget, I wrote *One for the Road* in 1984. It's taken me four years to write a 20 minute play. [Laugh.] I must have been doing something else during all this time.

MG: You've also been writing movies.

HP: I've written three scripts in the last two years, movies which all have to do, one way or another, with political states of affairs. *The Handmaid's Tale* – that's Margaret Atwood's projection into a possible United States 25 to 30 years from now. The one that's just been shot is *Reunion* by Fred Uhlman. He was a German painter who wrote this one novella, which is about Stuttgart in 1932, about a Jewish boy and a German boy who were great friends. The Jewish boy is sent away by his parents to New York and goes back to Germany 55 years later, and meanwhile his parents committed suicide and his best friend became a Nazi. The other one is an adaptation of *The Heat of the Day* by Elizabeth Bowen. It deals with a British officer who is working for the Germans; he believes the Germans are right.

MG: These are in contrast to your earlier screenplays, *The Servant*, *Accident*, *The Go-Between*, which may have had some political message but . . .

HP: *The Servant* is about the English caste system.

MG: *Turtle Diary* has no political message.

HP: No, *Turtle Diary* is about lonely people. But there's

a link between all these concerns in the end. Don't you think?

MG: A distinction could be made between your early plays and movies and your current ones.

HP: I cannot say that every work I've written is political. There's nothing political about *Landscape*. What the hell is political about *Old Times*? I would say, nothing. But I feel the question of how power is used and how violence is used, how you terrorize somebody, how you subjugate somebody, has always been alive in my work.

MG: There's a line on the book-jacket for *One for the Road* that says the play is a study of power and powerlessness. That's a pithy statement about the play.

HP: I think so. I approved that. The whole question of power and powerlessness again seems to be embodied in the relationship between the USA and Nicaragua. The extraordinary thing about good old Nicaragua is that it refuses to lie down and be trampled to death. It's a pitifully poor country, bankrupt, and yet they've not surrendered. In the last 40 years, we've been encouraged to believe that the evil exists on the other side of the Iron Curtain. Being encouraged to look 'over there,' we quite obviously draw a blank about what is happening in our lives. You have the rhetoric of the free, the Christian, the democratic, but underneath the rhetoric what you have is excrement, vomit, urine, blood, mutilation, horror, deprivation, poverty.

Let me tell you something. Mrs. Thatcher, the great Prime Minister, went to Turkey the other day to talk to another great prime minister. [Laugh.] A number of us through Amnesty International deposited a letter to 10 Downing Street asking her to discuss with the Prime Minister the situation of human rights in Turkey. In Turkey at the moment there are 30 writers in jail, which

73

is more than anywhere else in the world. When asked on television if she had discussed the question of human rights, she said, 'I am sure the Prime Minister is doing everything that is necessary.' What she actually did was to make a deal to build a third bridge over the Bosporus. That was a business trip. I'm going to pause for a moment, you'll be happy to hear, Mel, by simply saying, what the United States is saying in Central America is power is money and money is power. The U.S. policy in Central America seems to me to be profoundly disgusting and has been so for a very long time. And my country simply says yes whenever asked by your country, and vice versa.

MG: What's happened to your anti-Thatcher discussion group?

HP: It's extremely energetic. We meet in our house, but we could fill the Albert Hall – the letters we've received and the support we've had in this country. We are simply doing what we've set out to do, which is to have private meetings. We're acting as an independent body of citizens and have been scorned and derided for daring to think. We're going to continue to think and we're going to continue to meet and we're going to continue to argue and discuss.

MG: A lot of that scorn and derision came because many of you are artists.

HP: That's right. Scorn and Derision have traditionally been the weapons of the English establishment. 'You writers, you do terribly well, your taxes have been lowered, some of you have made a lot of money, what are you complaining about?' When I was in Nicaragua, I had an hour and a half alone with Ortega and one of the things he told me was that coffin-like boxes are kept by Sandinistas, to show the tourists, if there are any tourists. Under the Somoza regime, the peasants actually lived in those boxes. If you walk past Waterloo by the National Theatre and Festival Hall, just under the arches are box upon box. They're not slaves in the sense of Somoza, but they have no rights. They are the dispossessed and disenfranchised. They're totally forgotten, and when they're not forgotten they're brutalized. [Pause.] You see me coming to the whole question, which I know you want to do, of playwriting. I'm not writing about that. I can't write about that!

MG: Why not?

HP: Well, because I don't know how to. Anyway, what I would probably prefer to do is, A, talk about it to you, or in public context, or to make a documentary.

MG: Does the act of playwriting not interest you as much now as it did before?

HP: Yes, it does. But it's changed. My attitude toward my own playwriting has changed. The whole idea of a narrative, of a broad canvas stretching over a period of two hours – I think I've gone away from that forever. I can't see that I could ever encompass it again. I was always termed, what is the word, 'minimalist.' Maybe I am. Who knows? But I hope that to be minimal is to be precise and focused. I feel that what I've illuminated is quite broad – and deep – shadows stretching away.

MG: As much can be said in 20 minutes as could be said in two hours?

HP: Yes, but people don't necessarily agree. I was asked a very interesting question by a student at Sussex University. 'Can't you see a way of allying what you're doing now with characters as you used to write them, people called Meg and Max?' I said, 'I don't think I can any longer.'

MG: Isn't this a route followed by Beckett?

HP: That's true.

MG: Did you think about him when you were writing these plays?

HP: No. I must say there is one play of his that I think is a masterly encapsulation of this whole business. *Catastrophe*. There is only one man in the world who could have written that . . . I do admire Brecht more and more, including his poetry. I think he was a hell of a poet and a political mind of the greatest distinction. [Pause.] I don't think I could write a full-length play again, but who knows? I don't want to cut myself off from all experiences likely to come.

The great thing about doing *Mountain Language* by itself is, that's it! I assure you, it really works as an evening in the theatre. You can always go out and have a drink afterwards, or dinner . . . I would like to emphasize that I'm writing in the background of a government, which every day passes another law that strangles the life of the country. You know we used to have the Lord Chamberlain. I met him the other night, not the actual Lord Chamberlain but the fellow who used to do the real work. I remembered him very well. Lieutenant Penn. I happened to bump into him and we had a very amiable chat. He said, 'You used to come up to St. James's Palace.' I said, 'We certainly did.' He said, 'You couldn't say fuck, you couldn't say shit.' The word arse was on the cusp. That was negotiable. He said to me, 'Well, at least you knew where you were then, old boy,' and I said, 'You're too damn right.' Now there's a deep apprehension and fear on the part of media. Censorship is all over the place, and self-censorship. That's when it becomes insidious.

MG: Did they censor *The Birthday Party*?

HP: No, no words. You know I just acted in it last year on BBC television. I played Goldberg. A great cast: Joan Plowright, Colin Blakely, Julie Walters. [Pause.] Listen, I feel quite energetic. I certainly don't feel less energetic. Antonia and I play tennis a great deal. We're known as the Pinters who come from way back, because we always get off to a slightly bad start. A few weeks ago when we celebrated the first night of *Mountain Language* and Antonia's book, *The Warrior Queens*, which was published the same week, we had two heavy nights. We then played doubles at tennis. We suddenly found ourselves down love five. We were looking at each other rather bleakly and saying, well this seems to be it. It's a long time since we've been beaten six love. We took one game, then five three, five four, five all, and we won seven, five.

Our group is called the 20th of June because we met on the 20th of June. It's casual, but serious. [He takes the microphone of the tape recorder in his hands.] I'd like to record this: Those journalists who gave that kind of reception to this idea of serious people meeting to talk about serious subjects like the state of the country – I have absolute contempt for the lot of them.

MG: Is Tom Stoppard in the group?

HP: No. I like Tom Stoppard enormously, I respect and admire him. He made one of the most brilliant speeches I've ever heard, about censorship and freedom in England. This was seven or eight years ago. It was a wonderful speech and I wonder what he would say now. I haven't seen him for a while, but we're very attached. I believe that he's a conservative man. He's quite entitled. Not everyone who votes Conservative in England is representative of an Evil Empire.

MG: Simon Gray, writing about *One for the Road*, said the character of Nicholas was related to Max, Davies,

Goldberg and McCann. He said you would also find congenial company in Dickens' world, adding, 'But then Harold's always been a very English writer rather than the enigmatic European intellectual like Beckett, Kafka, etc. that academics and critics would like to turn him into. Like Dickens, he can make one laugh in panic.'

HP: I find what he says a great compliment. I also think it's accurate so far as I'm concerned. I feel English and I do believe the humour is English.

MG: Then he describes you directing *The Common Pursuit*, and says, 'Harold began by making a pronouncement about not wishing to make any pronouncements.'

HP: Don't forget that Simon is also a writer of fiction.

MG: Are you back at the National?

HP: I'm very much a supporter of the new regime. And for what it's worth, Peter Hall and I have been reconciled. I went to his farewell dinner and we've shaken hands.

MG: The last time we talked you said you wanted to come out of 'rooms'.

HP: Well, there's a room in *Mountain Language*, but there's also a corridor. What I was talking about was freeing myself.

MG: There was an article in a newspaper about the serious possibility of time travel. If you could time travel, where would you go?

HP: [He whistles.] I would find Elizabethan London pretty irresistible. I know about the dirt and stink and everything. My wife would probably laugh at me. I'd love to meet Webster, Tourneur, whoever the hell Tourneur was, not to mention Shakespeare. He'd have a few things to answer.

MG: He'd say, 'I don't write political plays. I simply write plays.'

HP: I suppose Shakespeare's dominated my life the way he's dominated many people's lives. We don't recover from Shakespeare. I acted Shakespeare as a young man. I'd like to do more acting. You know Tom Stoppard's story. When he was a drama critic in Bristol, the Evening Standard wanted a new political columnist, and he volunteered for the job. The editor asked him what was the name of the Foreign Minister. Tom paused and said, 'I said I was interested in politics, not obsessed with it.' That's how I feel about acting.

October 1989

[Silence, followed by audience laughter]

On the night of October 3, 1989, the private Pinter became public Pinter. In several previous appearances at New York's 92nd Street Y, he had held strictly to his text, a reading of poetry or excerpts from his plays. This time, he acted a scene from The Hothouse *and then performed the entire* One for the Road, *playing all the roles in both pieces. He acted to the fullest: he was funny, dramatic, malevolent and violent, at one point threatening an empty chair representing one of his characters.*

At Pinter's request, I participated in the event, introducing him to the audience, then after his performance joining him on stage in a conversation in which I posed questions and also selected questions from those submitted by members of the audience. The air was filled with emphatic pauses, and people responded vocally and with laughter. Pinter remained polite and in control, even as he escalated into one of his political discussions.

MG: When I heard the selection from *The Hothouse* followed by *One for the Road*, it seemed clear that this was a verification of what I consider to be the arc of your work. You've always been a political playwright. One can trace a serious interest in your art in the world of politics from *The Birthday Party* and *The Hothouse* all the way through to *One for the Road* and *Mountain Language*.

81

HP: I think in the early days, which was 30 years ago in fact, I was a political playwright of a kind. But I then took a break from being so for about 17 years. I wrote a lot of plays between 1970 and 1985 which can't be said to be political plays – things like *Old Times* and *Betrayal* and *Landscape* and *Silence*, which were concerned with memory and youth and loss and certain other things. They didn't concern themselves with social and political structures whereas the earlier plays did. I must say I chose to read the two tonight because it did strike me as quite interesting that in *The Hothouse* in 1959 there was a power crazy lunatic at the centre of this play, who in many ways was a farcical character although savage and alarming. Nevertheless, a creature that appeared to be larger than life. A nut! [Audience laughter.] And that play was full of jokes. You saw a little of it. My early work was I think full of games and jokes, but I think the distinction I would make between those plays then and these plays now is that I'm afraid that for me the joke is over. I can't see any more jokes, and I can't play any more games. I therefore find I am writing shorter and shorter pieces which are more and more brutal and more and more overtly naked.

MG: Simon Gray always seems to enjoy writing about you. In one piece, he said: 'Harold loves laughter in the theatre, especially when it is provoked by his own plays. The cathedral reverence with which they are sometimes received, thanks mainly to the industrious spadework of English departments and literary journals, must be exasperating.' Are you exasperated by the cathedral reverence which people bring to your work?

HP: In so far as I can detect it, yes I am. I made a terrible mistake when I was young, I think, from which I've never really recovered. I wrote the word 'pause' into my first play. [Laughter.] I really do believe that was a fatal error because people have been reading my plays and acting my plays most of the time concerned, really obsessed with this pause. I meant it merely as a natural break in the proceedings, or even a breath. [Pause.] But it's become something metaphysical.

MG: One of the questions from the audience is, 'What is the best thing you ever said with a pause?' [Audience laughter.] I detect a pause as you're waiting to answer.

HP: I have no favourite.

MG: I think we'll move on to the next question. Two years ago, you played Goldberg in a television production of *The Birthday Party*. As a young actor, you played Iago and the First Murderer in *Macbeth* and now we've just seen your Nicholas in *One for the Road*. Do you have a special affinity for such villainous roles?

HP: Definitely. Yes. I was in English rep as an actor for about 12 years. My favourite roles were undoubtedly the sinister ones. They're something to get your teeth into. I also started from a very early age in actually hating the audience. That's an attitude I preserved until this very day. With the exception, naturally, of this audience. It was very good to play sinister roles at an early age because you could frighten the audience. It was a continual conflict and tussle with the audience. I noticed tonight there were one or two latecomers and it took me back many many years when it was my habit to stare at latecomers, even while playing Iago. But of course I have become serene in my middle age.

MG: Serene?

HP: Serene, yes.

MG: Not immediately evident. How does it feel to enact your own plays? Does Pinter the playwright watch Pinter the actor? Is the director staring over your shoulder?

HP: I don't think so. I'm just aware of the peril that actors, to whom I take my hat off, go through every night. It's very salutary for a writer whether he has or has not been an actor to enter into that sea which is really going like that. [He rocks his hand.] There are no certainties in performing at all. You don't know what's going to happen next, although you try to plan. You have a curious structure available to you. But you can slip down so many keyholes, abysses, in the course of that journey. It really is an adventure. To sustain it is an extraordinary feat.

MG: Having been an actor, does that help you as a playwright? Is there a direct correlation?

HP: I've no idea really.

MG: I think we'll go to the next question: 'Sir, discuss intimidation.' I wouldn't know how to respond to that myself. Do you have a response? [Silence, followed by audience laughter.] I think we've seen enough intimidation already. The next question: 'Can the theatre change the world? Pause. How?'

HP: [Pause, smile]. Well, I'd prefer to go back to the question about intimidation. I think we are extremely intimidated by the countries in which we live. Certainly we are intimidated by dear old England. Many many people live a life of intimidation, even if they don't realize it. But many of them do, certainly the millions who have no money and are not only dispossessed but are effectively being disenfranchised as well by various governmental techniques and tactics. They are essentially citizens without a role, and they are undermined, bewildered and intimidated. This is to do with a very successful pattern of lies, which government actually tells to its citizens, and, I have to say, which is repeated in so much of the media. You're told that you're a happy man, it's a wonderful society, everything is fine. We're told that this is a free country. We're told that we live in a democracy. We're told that other people suffer various ills, various oppressions, of which we are free. And we say, that must be the case. I see it most strongly embodied in this country's relationship with Central America. [Applause.]

The actual facts simply do not correspond to the language used about those facts. What the language used by the media here and certainly the administration of this country, and echoed all along the line by the government of England, what the language does is debase itself. We're talking about a debased language in which the lie is simply automatic and quite persuasive and infinitely pervasive. It pervades the tradition in which we live, and certainly for the last 40 years this has been the case in what we call our Western democracies, in which – referring specifically to Central America – we are told that there is a totalitarian dungeon existing in Nicaragua, and democracies existing in El Salvador and Guatemala. I'm sure I'm not alone in knowing certain of the real facts. If I am alone and some of you would like to know the real facts, I'd be happy to tell you. Those are these. In the last 15 years, nearly 300,000 people have died in Guatemala, El Salvador and Nicaragua. This is brought about, in my view, by the foreign policy of this country.

While this has been going on, our attention has been drawn to the other side, what used to be called the Iron Curtain, now breaking down. I shall stop in a moment because I know you don't want me to give a sermon on this subject. But I just want to make one or two facts absolutely clear. I see myself not only as an actor and an entertainer but since you've been so kind to invite me here I'm also a citizen of the world in which I live. I take responsibility for that; I really insist upon taking responsibility and I understand my responsibilities quite precisely as trying to find out what the truth is. What I've found is that we're at the bottom of a blanket of lies, which unfortunately we are either too indifferent or too frightened to question. I'll leave it there for the moment.

MG: There's one other political question. 'Would Mr. Pinter comment on the relatively weak response by the English literary community to the Ayatollah's death sentence on Salman Rushdie. I know Mr. Pinter was an exception and did speak out, but what about his colleagues?'

HP: It's totally untrue. The English literary community has been very very strong indeed. There are all sorts of things happening. A public reading at that point was not considered to be the most helpful thing. English PEN which represents English writers and the writers union and all other bodies joined together in a body called Article 19. Many representations were made to the Muslim community, to the government. There has been infinite support for Salman Rushdie in England.

MG: I would like to go back to *One for the Road*, to discuss the genesis of that play. Was there one incident or image that sparked it off?

HP: The world which the play inhabits had not only been on my mind for many years but I had actually expressed it one way or another in the earlier plays. At the moment, the CSC Repertory are rehearsing two plays of mine, which open in a couple of weeks. One is *The Birthday Party*, which was written in 1957 I think. The other is my last short play, *Mountain Language*. Both of them have to do with oppression and the individual, and I think it is a very odd echo to find after all these years that both plays are finally referring to the same thing. So *One for the Road* has been around for a long time. There are bits of *One for the Road* in *The Birthday Party* itself.

But there was one specific thing which did actually cause me to begin the play. I wrote it in an absolute fury

86

one night after a party. I had met some young Turkish women. They were living in England. One of them worked in the Turkish embassy in fact. I asked them what they made of the torture, which is widespread to this very day in Turkey, our ally in NATO, by the way. Turkey had then and has now the worst human rights record in Europe, given Iran, and also has more writers in prison now than anywhere else in all of Europe. I asked these girls what they thought about the systematic and widespread torture that existed in Turkish prisons and police stations. They said, 'Well, they're probably Communists,' meaning the people who are being tortured. I was more or less speechless, for a change.

I actually left the room at that point, went back and wrote *One for the Road*. I just wrote it all in one night. It was interesting for me, to put it mildly, to try to find out what my imagination would find in response to that assertion on their parts, that because these people who were being arrested and tortured were apparently Communists, they deserved to be tortured and in fact killed. Later, when I went to Turkey on an extraordinary trip with Arthur Miller, we met people who had been badly tortured: writers, academics, trade union people. More to the point, we found their families had been destroyed. I remember the wife of a man who had been tortured had lost the power of speech. Her mind had been paralyzed through the experience of observing her husband in prison. Therefore, I related that to the kind of attitude these girls embodied, of rhetoric, nonsense, living in a fairy tale country where some people are saved and some people are punished, the good and the bad. That's why I wrote the play.

MG: What was the reason for having the villain and the victim have the same name, Nicholas and Nicky?

HP: I don't know.

[SILENCE, FOLLOWED BY AUDIENCE LAUGHTER]

MG: Just happened?

HP: Yes. I'm sure any writers here would agree. One of the remaining joys of writing, ever present, is that when the thing is really going [snaps his fingers], you surprise yourself. I suddenly found the boy's name was Nicky. It's as simple as that.

MG: Was Samuel Beckett's play *Catastrophe* an influence in writing it?

HP: No, it wasn't, but I think it's a wonderful play. I don't think I knew it at the time.

MG: Your next project is writing a screenplay of Kafka's *The Trial*. Why *The Trial* at this time?

HP: I read *The Trial* when I was a lad of 18, in 1948. It's been with me ever since. I don't think anyone who reads *The Trial* – it ever leaves them, although it can be curiously distorted by time. Speaking to a number of people, who remember having read it when they were young, they look back and think it's a political book. They rather tend to think it's like Arthur Koestler. In my view, it isn't at all. I admire Koestler, but I wouldn't be interested in writing a screenplay of *Darkness at Noon,* because it's so specifically of its time and place. But *The Trial* is not that case at all. I find it very difficult to talk about, except that it has been with me for 40 years, and I've had a whale of a time over the last few months entering into Kafka's world. The nightmare of that world is precisely in its ordinariness. That is what is so frightening and strong.

MG: And you certainly are aware of Orson Welles's film.

HP: Yes. Orson Welles was a genius but I think his film was quite wrong because he made it into an incoherent nightmare of spasmodic half-adjusted lines, images, effects in fact. As I said, I don't think Kafka is at all about affect, effect, but about something that happens on Monday, and then on Tuesday, and then on Wednesday and then right through the week. This man in *The Trial* is arrested one morning in his bed by two people and he is then let out, he goes to his job, a case is taking place. There seems to be a kind of implacable but invisible force and he is finally executed. The important thing about it is that he fights like hell all the way along the line. It reminded me of the shot in John Ford's film, The *Grapes of Wrath*, when the man is protecting his shack when the tractor comes up: 'If you go any further, I'll shoot your head off.' The fellow takes off his goggles and says, 'There's no point doing that because I'm going to knock your house down. I'm getting paid for that and if I don't do it there'll be another guy who will.' He says, 'I'll still knock your head off.' 'Then you'll have to shoot the other guy's head off. You've got to go to the bank in Oklahoma City, and you'll have to shoot all of them. Then you'll have to go to the bank in New York. How many people can you shoot?' He says, 'Get out of my damn way,' and he knocks the house down. One of the most terrible sequences in cinema, in a wonderful film. That's what Kafka's looking at: who do you shoot?

MG: Would you ever have considered turning *The Trial* into a play rather than a screenplay?

HP: No. I can't do that. I never adapted anything to the stage. It's not my thing. I enjoy cinema very much. I always have. Two things happened to me at a very early age. Naturally I fell in love, and I also found the cinema. They were actually two loves: cinema and girls – and sprinting, I think.

MG: What was the last one?

HP: Sprinting! I used to move fast in those days. But the

cinema was great, and always has remained so. I've enjoyed all my work in the cinema, without exception really. I think I'm very fortunate in that of course, because I know what normally happens to writers working in the film industry. I've been fortunate – in the people with whom I've worked.

MG: The one play of yours that has not been revived with any great frequency is *No Man's Land*. Clearly that's because of the identification with John Gielgud and Ralph Richardson. I wonder if it's not time for a major revival. Who would be in it? After watching your performance tonight, I thought, perhaps you as an actor-author might team up with another actor-author like John Osborne or Alan Ayckbourn. Has that possibility ever arisen?

HP: I'll bear that in mind. [Audience laughter.] The possibility has never arisen. The play was done in various countries like Germany, France and Italy, where two great actors in each country said, this is for us. I think actors are generally frightened of the play, simply because the ghost of Richardson and the live ghost of Gielgud are still very much around. There's no one to touch them.

MG: What other playwrights have you been influenced by?

HP: It's rather difficult to say. I started writing plays in 1957, when I was 27. Up to that point, I really hadn't seen many plays, apart from Shakespeare. I read Dostoevski and Kafka and Joyce and Hemingway. I knew O'Casey but I can't say I was influenced by him – and a little Strindberg. But I never asked myself that question. I can't answer it now.

MG: Are there any plans to produce your Proust screenplay?

HP: I'm afraid not. For the simple reason it's become so expensive over the years. It's not the kind of expensive picture that the film industry wants to do.

MG: How much of your character development is contrived and how much, if any, solely the result of initial impulse or image?

HP: I haven't the faintest idea.

MG: Do you read or talk your dialogue out loud when you're writing it?

HP: I never stop. If you were in my room, you would find me chattering away . . . I always test it, yes, not necessarily at the very moment of writing but just a couple of minutes later.

MG: And you laugh if it's funny?

HP: I laugh like hell.

MG: The last time we talked you said that you thought your attitude toward playwriting had changed, that you had gone away from 'the idea of a narrative of a broad canvas stretching over a period of two hours.' I wonder if you have had second thoughts about that statement.

HP: It isn't a matter up to me to reconsider. Actually, nothing would give me greater pleasure than to write any play, of whatever length. I don't think length is important anyway. The one thing about the act of writing is that it is essentially an act of freedom, as I understand it. It's great to write any way, if you can do it. I just find it more and more difficult.

MG: There is the question, what is full length? One might justify 20 minutes, if it gives the audience a full experience.

HP: It could be argued, and I'm sure a lot of people would argue strongly against it. They could quite properly argue that a 20 minute play, or a 30 minute play, doesn't allow the fullness and complexity of life to be given its full rein, and there may be something in that. I'm only concerned at the moment with accurate and precise images of what is the case. I can no longer write a play about a family and what happens to it, except that in *One for the Road*, I remind you, the man, woman and child are actually husband, wife and he's their child. Therefore, in a rather odd way, that play is about what happens to a family. Coming back to an earlier question, does the theatre affect the world in which we live, the answer must be, that little [fingers close together]. But that little is something, and I respect the power of the correspondence between theatre and audience. I must make it clear that I've always hated propaganda plays. I've walked out of more agit prop plays. Nevertheless, I still feel there is a role somewhere for a kind of work which is not in strict terms pursuing the normal narrative procedures of drama. It's to be found, and I'm trying to find it.

MG: Would you ever be inclined to write more directly about a political situation, for example, to write a play about Nicaragua?

HP: No. What I do about Nicaragua is make a lot of speeches about it and write quite a few articles about it, and, as you know, I'm the chairman of the arts for Nicaragua fund in Great Britain, and I make a damn nuisance of myself. That's what I do, and that's what I understand is my role as a citizen both of my country and of the world. I think to write a specific play about such a situation is not something I could possibly do.

MG: You're bringing back *The Homecoming* next year for the 25th anniversary production. Do you plan to make any revisions or re-evaluations? How do you feel about returning to the play?

HP: I feel very good about it. It's just been revived in Chicago by the Steppenwolf company and they've certainly not asked for any revisions. I think it stands up all right. It's very odd to think that play was done 25 years ago, in 1965, and both Peter Hall, who'll be directing it in London, and I will be celebrating our 60th birthdays next year. Triple anniversary.

MG: Here's a question from the audience. 'Have you ever wondered what draws you to write plays of darkness and psychological terror?' Are you filled with darkness and psychological terror? [Audience laughter.] You're smiling.

HP: No, I'm not filled with darkness and . . . I think we all have, and this is going to be a very profound remark, we all have a little bit of darkness within us.

MG: Said with a smile.

September 1993

'Even old Sophocles didn't know what was going to happen next'

The opening of Moonlight at the Almeida Theatre began what was to be one of the most salutary weeks of Pinter's career. Several days later, the playwright presented his papers – all his extant manuscripts of 26 plays, 17 screenplays and sketches, prose and poetry – on a long-term loan to the British Library. In accepting the Pinter papers at a festive luncheon, Sir Anthony Kenny, the chairman of the library's board, said that the generosity was unprecedented. The 'Deposit of the Archives' was followed by the reopening on the West End of Pinter's compelling production of David Mamet's Oleanna (starring David Suchet). Surrounded by these visible signs of his success, Pinter was in a celebratory mode.

The focus was on Moonlight, a portrait of family relationships undermined by years of divisiveness. Although it runs only 85 minutes without intermission, it is a complete, richly textured play. At the centre is a father on his deathbed, raging against the night of dying, a character superbly played by Ian Holm, himself returning to the stage after a long absence. As with all Pinter, Moonlight is filled with mystery. Is the daughter, a wraithlike poetic figure, a ghost? Are the grandchildren imaginary? Why do the two sons refuse to return *home? The play is a return to earlier Pinter as well as a step into previously uncharted dramatic territory, as a confrontation with questions of mortality.*

At noon two days after the opening, Pinter greeted me at the door of his study for the first of a series of conversations. Over lunch in a nearby restaurant we talked about the origins of the play.

MG: How did you come to write *Moonlight*?

HP: I started it last December. I was acting in *No Man's Land*. It may have been just saying those words every night, going on the stage and getting the sense of the language that touched something off. I was writing away in my study one day, and I suddenly said to myself, 'I have been here before; I have been with this character before.'

MG: Meaning Andy [the character played by Ian Holm].

HP: Yes. On the side of my study, there's a shelf, with a lot of scripts and papers and things. It's comparatively tidy and ordered at the moment, but at that time it was pile upon pile of stuff. I hadn't shifted it into shape for months. And I knew that somewhere under these piles there were a few yellow pads which I had put there, many years ago, and I became like a wild, mad composer, throwing these scripts and papers all over the place, to burrow into this, to find these yellow pages. And finally there they were. They went back to 1977. The image was of a man dying. I do tend to throw quite a lot of things away when they are not working but I never threw this out. It really wasn't very good, but there were certain elements of it which have remained exactly the same in the play. I had forgotten about it but it stayed with me.

MG: Did any words in the original go into the play?

HP: Some did. There was a kind of a snatch of a conversation between two men, which I had also written more or less the same time but totally disconnected to Andy. And he wasn't called Andy either. He was called A, I think. The other men were called A and B, too, but they were totally different.

MG: Do you know why you couldn't complete the earlier version, what left you adrift?

HP: When I read it now, I find it to be very crude. I wasn't getting anywhere with it. You know that line in the play, 'farting Annie Laurie down a keyhole', I think that was what was really happening to me. I remember, by the way, my German translator, she's Marianne Frisch, Max Frisch's widow. Her English is perfectly fluent, but she did say one thing. She said 'I am very confused by one sentence, what is 'farting Annie Laurie down a keyhole'?' I said 'Which part of the sentence are you referring to?' It was actually Annie Laurie. I explained that Annie Laurie is an old Scottish . . . you know it? . . .

Although I knew it wasn't getting anywhere, I didn't throw it away. And I think once or twice over the years, I opened it. It's in a little folder. I would come across it, open it, take one look and just shut the folder. But I never threw it away. The thing was, I was writing the play without using those yellow pages. The play was taking its own form.

Then we went away for a couple of weeks on holiday and I worked very very intensely, feverishly. We were in Mauritius, in the Indian Ocean, way away. I always like to work on holiday. I hired an old manual typewriter, prehistoric really, and I did the drafts on that typewriter. It made a hell of a noise, this typewriter banging and clanking way into the night. I like siestas, for an hour, but I had no such thing in Mauritius. I had no time for siestas. That's why I say 'feverishly.' I couldn't stop. [Pause.]

MG: With other plays, an image or a line of dialogue triggered off your imagination. Was there something specific in *No Man's Land* that started you on *Moonlight*?

HP: Well, I think it was just a very simple question of an image of a man in bed, dying, and his wife was in the room. I knew he was a man of considerable vigour, and I am pretty sure that the line 'Where are they?' [meaning his sons] was central to the whole. It was a question of children who weren't there.

MG: Do you remember what made you see the man in bed?

HP: One moment the man in bed was not there, and the next moment he was there. There was one speech in *No Man's Land*, which I as Hirst delivered, the speech about the photograph album. I'll just give you the idea:

'I might even show you my photograph album. You might even see in it a face which might remind you of your own; of what you once were. You might see faces of others, or in shadow, or cheeks of others, turning or jaws or backs of necks, or eyes, dark under hats, which might remind you of others whom once you knew and you thought long dead but from whom you will still receive a sidelong glance if you can face the ghost. Allow the love of a ghost. They possess all that emotion, trapped. Bow to it. Assuredly it can never release them but who knows what relief it may give to them? Who knows how they may quicken in their chains and their glass jars? Do you think it cruel to quicken them when they are fixed, imprisoned? No, no. Deeply, deeply they wish to respond to your look, to your touch, and when you smile their joy is unbounded. So I say to you, tender the dead as you would yourself be tendered in what you would describe as your life.'

Now, that's the speech and there was something about that sense of death, and ghosts, and the dead who are alive in us that I think quickened something in me in relation to *Moonlight*. There was always an absolute hush in the house during that speech, so the audience's awareness or interest in that idea of the dead being present woke me up too.

MG: Was there anything else that fed into that?

HP: Well, it's a question of when the girl, Bridget, arrived in my mind; because I believe that she is dead, I always understood her to be dead in the play. So therefore she was the embodiment of all this; this idea of the dead being present. I don't take notes of when characters appear. I don't say to myself, 'At 11 o'clock on Tuesday morning the 18th, Bridget suddenly appeared.' I find her; she is there. The idea of Bridget was the essential element. In my own view, she is the crux of the play, because she informs everything. I just can't explain it, I just feel that she is the very centre of the play, and she is much missed by all her family, including the boys.

MG: And there are no grandchildren.

HP: There are no grandchildren. Absolutely not. To anyone who cares to listen to the play that is pretty evident.

MG: Is the younger son dying?

HP: I don't think he is literally dying, but he makes it quite clear that he doesn't want to get out of that bed. So that's another kind of death. I think the fellow's just having a kind of nervous breakdown. I think it's a common condition for a lot of young men; perhaps even

99

more young men than young women. But I'm not an authority on the subject. The image of a fellow of his age, middle twenties, just not wanting to get out of bed, I think is something we know quite a lot about.

MG: This is your first full-length play in 15 years. Can you say what enabled you to overcome your writer's block?

HP: I really would like to say something about this question of a writer's block. You're quite entitled to call it a writer's block, and a lot of people have been talking about a writer's block. But the fact is, I have written – whether people like them or not, or think they're 'too short' – I have actually written six plays since 1978. I have also written seven screenplays, including *The French Lieutenant's Woman* and *The Trial*. Actually eight, including *The Remains of the Day*, which we'll come to later, so it's eight screenplays. Now these screenplays, I don't just transcribe the novel; otherwise you might as well do the novel. In other words, these are acts of the imagination on my part!

As for the plays, I believe that, in their own ways, they are works of substance. If you write a poem, it really doesn't matter whether the poem is two pages long or four lines. I think this whole question of length has become an obsession.

MG: Let me take back 'writer's block', but I want to read what you said to me in 1988: 'My attitude towards my own playwriting has changed, the whole idea of a narrative, of a broad canvas stretching over two hours, I think I've gone away from that forever. I can't see that I can ever encompass it again.' You said that you could no longer write full-length plays with characters named Meg and Max. Now it's back, and back in abundance. The question is how?

HP: Well, yes, it's back – I know what you're saying – but it's back in a very different form. I don't think I would ever be able to write *The Homecoming* again. *The Homecoming* is a play that I really think did find its form and pleases me. But I could never do that again. The narrative in *Moonlight* takes a very different form from anything I have ever written. If it resembles anything, it's possibly a short play I wrote years ago, *Silence*, in which there were three areas, as it were.

MG: It seemed clear five years ago that you were not prepared, or not able, to sit down and write a play that would deal with some of the things this play deals with, as *The Homecoming* and *Old Times* dealt with families and memories. They're different plays with different forms but with real people on stage, going through something the audience can readily identify with. The plays that came in between were very political, very terse, very pointed towards one direction. Whether it runs 85 minutes or two hours, this is a full rich play with real people on stage.

HP: And a range of experience, you mean? I accept that.

MG: Something allowed you, or forced you to sit down and create it, despite the fact that you said this would probably never happen again.

HP: Well I think you have put that very clearly. I won't hide the fact that I'm very excited about writing this play, and I appreciate that it possesses a range of experience and variety of references that I haven't really been doing much of over the last few years. And you're right. The short plays on the whole tended to focus on one thing, with varying degrees of success, but *Moonlight* is doing something else.

MG: The themes are there but dealing with a readily identifiable personal situation.

HP: I agree. There is a serious, clear distinction to be made. It's touching upon the lives of people in a more flexible and less rigorous way. *One for the Road* is about torture. And *Mountain Language* is about an army, and victims. *Party Time* is about a bunch of shits and a victim. All these are about power and powerlessness, those plays and *The New World Order*, which I don't even call a play. It's a sketch. But it does embody a lot of these concerns, in the sense that the image of one man sitting blindfold and two men about to torture him, possessing absolute power, the man blindfolded possessing no power whatsoever, sums all that up. So I agree with you, there is a substantial difference between those plays and *Moonlight*. I used the word rigorous just now. Those plays were pretty rigorous, and the attitude towards the characters was pretty rigorous. In *Moonlight*, I think I am more open to character.

MG: Do you think of it as a political play as well?

HP: I don't.

MG: The play seems to me to be more personal, rather than political. Would you go along with that?

HP: I think I would go along with that. I would agree that it is more personal, in the sense you're using the word, but I'm not sure that I can expand upon that.

MG: How much of the play might subconsciously derive from your own experience as the son rather than as the father; as a child growing up, in relation to your parents.

HP: That's very interesting. For the last 20 years or so I have had the most wonderful relations with my parents. My mother died last October, at the age of 88, and my father is still going very strong at the age of 91. I went down to see him a couple of days ago. He lives in Brighton. His mind is as clear as a bell, and he's quite a character. We're very close. He's got a lot of jokes up his sleeve, one or two quite good ones too. They were married for 66 years, and he's now very lonely. It's only his legs that are weak. Otherwise he's fine.

But going back, to be almost 63 and have a father of 91 is rather extraordinary. My adolescence and youth were a very different story indeed. My father was a man of considerable authority when he was young. I was a pretty rebellious young man. Don't forget I was also a conscientious objector in 1948, when I was 18, and was prepared to go to prison, which didn't go down very well with my mother and father. They were very solid, very respectable, Jewish, lower middle class people. My mother kept what is called an immaculate house, she was a wonderful cook, and all that. There was a very strong family sense altogether. But suddenly to have a Jewish boy going to prison for some idea about not wanting to join the army – it was a great shock to the system of the whole family! Nevertheless I didn't, as you know, go to prison. I had two trials and the magistrate fined me, which he had the right to do under the civil law because I was under 21. My father paid the fine both times, and he had to really find the money, too. It wasn't easy. But I took my toothbrush along with me to the trial. There was a considerable tension in my own youth. There's no question about that. I then married out of the religion too, which wasn't too popular.

MG: During the war you were sent away from London?

HP: Oh yes. Not for a long time. Just for about a year I went to Cornwall, and my mother and I later on went somewhere else. I spent a great deal of time in London during the war, but I was away, as were a lot of other children, in the very early days of the war, 1939, 1940. Children were evacuated.

MG: Was that a very traumatic experience?

HP: It was – very traumatic. At that time I was only nine or 10. I missed my parents. We missed each other very much. My father was an air raid warden in London. Once or twice they came down to Cornwall. A few years ago, I met again a fellow who was a boy with me in Cornwall. We stayed at this castle. His parents and baby sister were killed in one fell swoop by a bomb in London, and I remember very well I was with him when we got the news. It was very difficult to appreciate what death was. At nine, to hear that your parents and sister are dead; he couldn't take it in.

MG: The bantering of the sons in *Moonlight* reminded me of the bantering of the young men in your novel *The Dwarfs*. I assume that was a variation of what you were going through at that age.

HP: I hadn't actually thought of that, but I think it's true.

MG: Was that novel your first writing?

HP: Well no, my first writing was poems. In my teens I wrote hundreds of poems.

MG: Some people think you were an actor on tour who sat down and wrote *The Room* and became a playwright. The truth is that you were writing before.

HP: Oh yes. As Jake says in *Moonlight*, I was writing poems before I could read, before I was born. I was writing, I should think, at the age of 12 or 13. Then I wrote *The Dwarfs* in the late forties, early fifties. I've still got the actual manuscript of *The Dwarfs,* which is going to the British Library. They are all going. They've got the whole damned thing – apart from *Moonlight*, which I still have myself. I will give that to them, too. Actually, they haven't got the whole damned thing, because I've lost one or two things that I wrote, such as the original of *The Birthday Party*. I think when I was leaving my previous house, I left two or three boxes in my study there, and they disappeared. They include *The Birthday Party*, *The Room*, *The Dumb Waiter* and *A Slight Ache*. And then idiotically I sold the manuscript of *The Caretaker* to Indiana University about 30 years ago.

MG: Perhaps you needed the money.

HP: Not after *The Caretaker*. I was totally broke until *The Caretaker*. It's a mystery why I sold it. But I still have another draft that the British Library has.

MG: Do you consider *Moonlight* a breakthrough?

HP: It's like opening a door, and you suddenly realize you're on a plain of gold. There's a light coming in. I don't want to sound mystical about it. I think there's no question what excited me was the image of one family dislocated but very much part of each other.

A German director who's done a lot of my plays asked me about the set. He said, 'Why are the beds so close to each other?' I said, 'Well, you can do it any way you like. It just says there are two separate locations.' The space between two people, the emotional distance, could be a space of miles and miles and miles. You might as well as be on the moon. What I love about the design is the awful closeness. They seem to be so near, and they're not. They're thousands of miles away. The boys will never come. But I do believe there are echoes.

MG: It must have been a real turning point when Bridget appeared.

HP: Oh, yes. Suddenly, through her I was inhabiting a totally different perspective. In the very first speech of the play, she's talking about going downstairs. She appears to be alive. To me, she's dead.

MG: What happened to her?

HP: I don't know. I mean that absolutely frankly. All I know is she's dead. You know, I've been taken to task quite a lot for saying something like that, like 'I don't know.' But I don't. There are a number of things I don't know about my own work. I cannot answer every question. As I've said, I don't write theses, I write plays. The way I work, the way things come to me, images, either verbal or visual, just arrive. I saw her. I found her. I saw a girl of 16. Other people got older; she stopped.

MG: There are emanations of Beckett in *Moonlight*. When the daughter is pacing, I thought of *Footfalls*.

HP: You're right. Well, as a matter of fact that was entirely David Leveaux [the director]. It wasn't me. David Leveaux and Claire Skinner [who plays Bridget] between them. They found it. They showed it to me, and I thought it was very good, very telling. I didn't think of Beckett at the time, but you are absolutely right about *Footfalls* coming to mind.

MG: Did you think of Beckett when you were writing the play?

HP: No, I can't say that I did. If I had, I am sure that might have had a rather bad effect. If I suddenly thought 'This is like Beckett', it might have stopped me dead in my tracks. But I had no time to think about anyone, really, or anything. I just had to grasp the nettle.

MG: Did the play change much as you wrote it?

HP: Well, I worked very hard at it. There were a number of drafts, changes indeed.

MG: Were you aware of the ending as you began the play? Did you know the other couple would come on stage?

HP: No. I didn't know they were going to come on stage at any time, until they suddenly appeared. I think once one of them had come on there was another one that had to come on. I had no idea how the play was going to end or that these characters, Maria and Ralph, were going to appear. But they just did. It's always been like that in my experience of writing. At the beginning of *Old Times*, when A and B were speaking, there was a C in the background, standing there all the time. I knew that, but. I didn't know who she was. I knew it was a female. If I look at *The Homecoming,* I must have known that this couple were going to come back from America. I had to know that. But in a way I didn't know at exactly what point they would appear or what they were going to do. When they walked into that room, I didn't know what was going to happen.

MG: But that's the core of the play – what happens after they arrive.

HP: Yes, but I didn't know that it was. And this applies generally. In *Moonlight* I didn't know what was going to happen. There were three things I knew in *Moonlight*. I knew there were two boys and there was Bridget and there was Andy. But I didn't know what was going to happen between all those people; how they were going to reflect each other, except I knew a little more about Andy than anybody else. I knew he was just raging a good deal of the time.

MG: How close are you to Andy? He seems very alone.

HP: Not only alone, but he seems to deny the existence of more or less anybody else. He says at one point, 'Nothing ever happened.' He denies the existence of his own life, except he's so contradictory that he's also asserting it all the time. I like Andy. I think Andy's a long, long way from a dead person. Look, in a way I do feel very close to him. And incidentally I'm thrilled that Ian Holm has come back to do this. It gives me enormous pleasure.

MG: What do actors add to a play?

HP: There's a question of rhythm. I remember the very first time I went to New York for an American production of one of my plays, *The Collection* and *The Dumbwaiter,* directed by Alan Schneider, with Jimmy Ray, Jim Patterson, Henderson Forsythe and Patricia Roe. In '63 or '64. I remember the actors were twisting themselves into real knots about the meaning of the bloody lines and so on, in *The Collection* particularly. I remember saying at the time, 'Why don't you just say the line emphasizing such and such a word rather than thinking and thinking. Just say the line. I recommend this emphasis. It will come and you'll feel OK, really.' They looked me as if I was mad. I was going the other way round. I was saying that the music and the rhythm will tell you what you mean. You can work yourself into the ground, and you won't ever get anywhere unless you get the precise emphasis, and then the sense of the sentence will come clear. And what I did get here, in this production, with Ian Holm, is his sense of rhythm and the shape of the language. He puts on my shoe and it fits! It's really very gratifying. But I also have to say that David Leveaux has a wonderful ear as a director. He's a very delicate explorer.

MG: This is the first new play of yours that he's done.

HP: Yes. He did *Betrayal* and *No Man's Land* in which he had the author as one of the actors. Believe me, that was all right. He didn't have any problems with me.

MG: Lenny [in *The Homecoming*] and now Andy, that's a long stretch of time and a great difference of character for one actor.

HP: Yes, Ian was a great Lenny too. What a season he had then. He was Henry V and then of course Richard III. It's wonderful that he's back. This company is very pleasing for me because I've either acted or worked with all of the actors with the exception of Michael Sheen – the fellow in the bed – and Claire Skinner. But the rest of them, all of them . . . Jill Johnson and I were in rep together, you know, in 1955, in Colchester. Douglas Hodge was of course in *No Man's Land*. And this is the third time I've worked with Edward de Souza. Anna Massey was in two of my short plays, *A Kind of Alaska* and *Family Voices* at the National. Then she and I did *A Kind of Alaska* on radio.

MG: I was curious about your days in rep touring with Anew McMaster. How important was that in terms of leading you into theatre?

HP: Well, sure it was important. You read my *Mac*?

MG: Yes, and also saw the photographs by Pauline Flanagan of the troupe.

HP: Oh yes, they're remarkable, aren't they? I hadn't seen them for years and to suddenly see those tinkers, and the whole sense of touring actors. You were almost going to bed with a sheep next to you.

MG: Instead of turning you off theatre, it turned you on?

HP: Oh yes. Mac was a hell of a fellow. And can you imagine doing that sort of stuff every night? For a young actor to be introduced to the theatre by playing in *Hamlet, Oedipus Rex* – and being part of *Julius Caesar* and *Othello* in one week. You do four plays and then, as a bit of light relief, *The Importance of Being Earnest*. And *Rope*. Mac had to have a couple of nights off. I played *Rope* with Patrick Magee – and *The Importance of Being Earnest*. Patrick Magee was the most unlikely

Algernon I've ever come across in my life! [He laughs.]
But it had tremendous vitality and freedom.

MG: When you were touring, what were audiences like?

HP: We're talking of over 40 years ago, but my memory
is that they were terrific. The Shakespearean tragedies
were given very directly and were received very
directly. These were mainly country audiences. I never
played in Dublin. We played in Cork in a theatre that
burned down, called the Cork Opera House, a wonderful
theatre. It had a backstage bar, so actors could pop in
and have a drink while the show was running. We were
doing *Lady Windermere's Fan*, and I was playing Lord
Windermere. Joe Nolan came on one night wearing a top
hat, tails, white tie, a monocle, cloak and carrying a
silver walking stick; in other words, dressed to the nines.
He walked up to me on stage, in front of the full house,
and said in a very very quiet voice, under his breath,
'I'm totally pissed, say something!' I said, 'Ah! Lord
whatever-his-name-was, you've been I should imagine
to the Garrick.'

There was a beautiful theatre in Waterford, the Theatre
Royal, where Kean played. I went back there once. We
did a film called *Langrishe, Go Down*, which was shot
in Waterford about 15 years ago. I went into the theatre,
which was closed. I stood on the stage and I
remembered exactly the position I had stood when I
played Iago to Mac's Othello, which was one of the
great thrills of my life. I could have done the whole play.
One of the greatest moments of theatre I have ever
experienced was when Iago is probing Othello and he
goes slightly too far. He says about Cassio lying with
Desdemona, and I think Othello says 'With her? On
her?' And Iago says, 'With her, on her, as you will.'
When I said, as Iago, 'With her, on her, as you will,'
Mac turned, and the next moment he was strangling me
as he said the line, 'Villain, be sure thou prove my wife

a whore.' It was the most incredibly dramatic gesture. In fact I can still feel his hand round my throat!

MG: He let you play Hamlet for one performance. Where was that?

HP: In a convent, at a matinee. Afterwards I said to him, 'How was it, Mac?' He played the gravedigger. He said, 'Very good, but be a little more compassionate with your mother. You are very hard, very hard.' As a young man I wasn't going to go in for this romanticism with my mother.

MG: Later you were with Donald Wolfit's company. Was Ronald Harwood there at the time?

HP: Yes, he was 18.

MG: Was he the dresser?

HP: Yes.

MG: What were you acting in?

HP: I was the Second Murderer and Ross in *Macbeth* and also one of those two in *Merchant of Venice*.

MG: And Harwood was writing in the dressing room?

HP: I should think so. By the way, there is one story I have to tell you, Alan Ayckbourn came down and gave a lecture in London a few months ago, and he told a story – I wasn't there. He said that in 1959 he was a very young actor at Scarborough. He said this mad young author came up from London to direct his play, *The Birthday Party*, in Scarborough, at the Theatre in the Round – which I did. That was me. Alan said he had no idea what was going on in this play, and he said to me, 'I wonder if I could ask you a few questions about my character. Where do I come from? Can you tell me something about my background? For example, where would I have gone to school?' And this fellow, Harold Pinter, put his glasses up on his nose and said, 'Mind your own business!' Apparently this brought the house down at this lecture.

Incidentally, Jason Robards and Christopher Plummer are going to do *No Man's Land* in New York. David Jones is directing it [at the Roundabout]. I thought I'd go for a few days to be available for any questions. I've never met Jason Robards. He's been in two of my movies. He's in *The Trial,* and he's also in a film which has been very little seen, *Reunion,* directed by Jerry Schatzberg. It passed as if nothing had ever happened. I really can't fathom that, you know, because it's a really intelligent and delicate piece of work. Jason Robards gives a totally understated performance. I admire it tremendously. So I look forward to meeting him.

MG: Which part is he going to play?

HP: My part! He's playing Hirst.

MG: After you wrote *Moonlight,* what did you do with it next? Did Antonia read it?

HP: She did more than read it. I did something on holiday which I have never actually done in my whole life, either with my first wife or Antonia, which was to read aloud the drafts, in stages. Before, I had only done that with the finished play. But in this case it was midway. And I invited her to say whatever the hell she wanted to say, which I have also never done before.

She was wonderful. One thing she said was that she felt there was an absence of something, which was a sense of Bridget with her brothers, a sense of their life together. I acted on that.

112

MG: When did the title come?

HP: After I had finished it. I said, 'This is called *Moonlight*. That's it.' And Antonia said, 'Right.' Then I sent it to David Leveaux and to Ian MacDiarmid and Jonathan Kent [at the Almeida Theatre], and of course my agent, Judy [Judy Daish had become his agent after the death of Jimmy Wax]. So everything came together, and off we went. It really has been quite a busy year. I finished it and gave it to them in something like February. I was already planning to direct *Oleanna,* which then went ahead in May. So these two things have been running in a sense in tandem.

MG: Years ago, you would send your plays to Beckett. How many people receive copies of your plays now?

HP: It's called a mailing list! I do send them to more people. I feel my life has become much more open since Antonia and I have been together, which is now almost 18 years. Antonia and I have now been together as long as our first marriages. I think through my present marriage I have become more open so I send my plays to more people and I say more and irritate more people than I ever did, and so on.

MG: In the '60s, and thereafter, there was a certain secretive quality about the work and about you. Less so today.

HP: That's true. I will say one thing now. I knew perfectly well that *The Birthday Party* and *The Dumb Waiter*, in my understanding then, were to do with states of affairs which could certainly be termed political, without any question; not to mention *The Hothouse*. Of course I didn't bring that out till later. But *The Hothouse* couldn't be more political. And Goldberg and McCann, I knew who they were and what they were up to.

MG: But the critics and the audience didn't know.

113

HP: No. Nor did I, as it were, tell them. I didn't ever say. I sort of denied generally.

MG: During this time when you did not write a full-length play, you did some acting. Did that have an effect on the writing of this play?

HP: Well I think it did. It's rather difficult to describe how this actually manifested itself, or rather the correspondence, the relation between one thing and another. The question of using language every night, really having to use it and go with it, was very very strong and I am sure it somehow quickened my mind.

MG: If you had not appeared in *No Man's Land* you might not have broken through?

HP: Well, that's all speculation. That's the path I did not tread. The path I did not tread was the path of not acting. It so happened I did act.

MG: Were there any changes in *Moonlight* during rehearsal?

HP: Yes, a great cheer went up in rehearsal from the whole cast when Ian Holm gets the bottle and says, 'Bollocks to the lot of them, bugger them all!' and pours himself a drink. I said I loved the way he was doing it. He was raising his glass like this, and I said, 'I really like that, it's as if you're saying 'Cheers!' and he said, 'I often feel I'm saying 'Cheers!', and I said, 'Say it!' – which he did. The whole cast just broke up actually – my god!, what's happening? I'm delighted he says 'Cheers!' and I love it. So at the next reprinting, I'll put 'Cheers! (courtesy of Ian Holm).'

MG: Ian said Paul Rogers saw the play. He was carrying a cane, and Ian suggested that he use a cane when he got out of bed. You and David Leveaux said no.

HP: I believe that Max [Rogers' role in *The Homecoming*] and Andy have something in common. Vigour.

MG: But one is dying and one is alive.

HP: That's true. That's the difference. I think that Andy is a much more subtle character than Max, but they both have energy.

MG: One's a butcher, one's a civil servant.

HP: Yes. But you can get subtle butchers too. Max is certainly not one of them! And you can get pretty brutish civil servants. In this case I think Andy is another kind of intelligence, but they have a language in common, a mode of using language. They sort of recognize each other somewhere along the line. Honestly, I don't sit and think about my own work, I really don't. But since you ask it, I do perhaps feel that there is some common factor in a lot of these central characters that I have written over the years, like Goldberg and Davies and Max and Andy. There's a lineage there, they're all pretty gross, one way or the other. The thing is, they seem to relish their own grossness.

MG: Is there an original for all those characters?

HP: You're looking for a long lost uncle, or something?

MG: Some person who inspired all the Maxes and the Andys.

HP: [Pause.] No, there was no one specific. In the East End of London, where I grew up, it was a very very lively, active kind of world; a lot of people who talked a lot. They talked very fast. It was during and after the war, and there was a sense of release. People were just talking very fast. You know this country has changed a great deal. It has now become, for a clear set of reasons,

I think, progressively more sullen, more bewildered, more secret, certainly more aggressive and more alarming. The violence, the pressure, there's a force here – it's in so many other places but it's here too – which explodes in random areas. It explodes in prisons, as you know. There could be an explosion very easily here because of some of the inner city areas which suffer from dreadful poverty. And there are a lot of people now being thrown out of mental homes. They're closing down, with no care whatsoever.

But when I was young – I'm not saying things were perfect, because they certainly weren't – there was a kind of release after the war – which also released all sorts of other things including fascism. There was a revival of fascism here in 1945 and 1946, although we were supposed to have defeated fascism. There used to be public meetings and all that when I was still at school. Very violent. With the Labour government after the war, there was a lot of optimism, and wonderful things were done. The health service, for instance, now more or less in tatters, but it was an extraordinary thing, to provide a health service for the whole country. It had never happened before. There was a kind of vitality in the world I grew up in.

MG: In contrast to some playwrights, you don't write directly from your life.

HP: No. The only time I wrote from, hardly from my life but from an actual very specific reference was *A Kind of Alaska*, which was to do with Oliver Sacks' book. That was a direct, specific connection. It actually inspired me to investigate that kind of idea, which was not my idea but his.

MG: People are interested in what you say, and in what you do not say?

HP: I'll give you one example of something that happened here which is very much to the point. *The Trial* was about to open here. The BBC had financed a certain amount of it. And the same week as the film opened here, they were showing the Orson Welles film on BBC television. So everyone – the director, the producer – said, 'What the hell's going on here?' It was an extraordinary decision for someone to do this. Whatever anyone thinks about the Orson Welles film, it's an Orson Welles film, and to show it to millions of people on television the same week . . . Now, I was busy directing *Oleanna* at the time, and I said absolutely nothing to anybody, not a word. I carried on with my work. I woke up one morning, to read on the front page of The Times – there was a little photograph of me, at the top of The Times, with a caption saying something like 'Pinter indignant. See page 6.' On page 6 there was a very big photograph of me, in a suit, and it looked as though I was addressing a press conference. I don't even know where the damned photograph came from. Not only had I not addressed a press conference, I hadn't spoken to anyone. And the headline of the piece actually said, in big black letters, 'Pinter irate.'

I thought, 'What the fuck's going on here?' So I wrote a short letter to The Times saying, 'So help me god, I ain't spoken to a soul; give a guy a break,' and I wrote to the Press Council. There is a Press Council, believe me, not that it's worth very much here. For complaints, you know. I just wrote, 'I do think I need an apology from The Times . . . for a total invention.' They wrote a stalling letter back saying, 'Oh, we're sure there's been some misunderstanding,' and I said, 'There's been no misunderstanding.' To cut a long story short, they printed my letter, but I still wanted an apology. You can't just print a letter without giving an explanation and finally The Times did write. There were two letters and the final one said, 'We apologize.' It's now on record at the Press Council. It was a total bloody invention. It was assumed that I was irate but I wasn't anything. So in a way, they've created another character, another man.

MG: He should have been outraged.

HP: Yes. He was bound to be outraged. Well, let's say he was outraged. But that's the kind of persona I've been given around here; that I'm always 'outraged'. Sometimes I am outraged, but, you know, not every day of the week.

MG: Ian Smith [an Oxford don who plays cricket on Pinter's team] speaks about the roots of Joyce and Eliot in your work.

HP: I certainly believe I'm part of a tradition which undoubtedly includes Joyce and Eliot. You know, I read *Ulysses* every night when I go to bed. If I'm going to read for a couple of minutes, I have *Ulysses* by my side. It gives me great, great joy. It makes me laugh.

MG: Would you have liked to have known Joyce?

HP: Oh yes. Don't forget, I directed his one and only play, *Exiles*. It was one of the quietest productions ever known. It was hushed. I eschewed all rhetoric, which the language, or some of it, could lead you to fall into.

MG: Did you ever talk to Beckett about Joyce?

HP: Yes. I talked to him about that production. He wrote to me about it. He never saw it because he never went to the damned theatre but he was very, very interested and delighted I was doing it. I talked to him at length about it, because I was convinced it was a real goer on stage, whereas Ezra Pound said, 'This doesn't work, it's totally unstageable.' I printed that in the programme. I'd have loved Joyce to have popped in and seen it. I think he would have liked it. I would love to have had a drink with Joyce, and with Proust. But I never got around to it.

On 10 September 1993, we met for a late lunch. Pinter had just come from a memorial at the Chilean Embassy, and began talking about the event of the day.

HP: This is the 20th anniversary of the coup in Chile, consequently the 20th anniversary of the death of Victor Jara, the very, very popular Chilean folksinger who was a strong supporter of the Allende government. He was murdered in the stadium, and his wife, Joan Jara, is back in Chile now. We were delivering a wreath to the new Chilean ambassador to commemorate the death and its significance. There's considerable tension over there. The military don't want to know, they don't want any of these murderers to be investigated, just to be pardoned. The same thing applies in other countries as well – Argentina, Brazil, Uruguay; there are amnesties. I went in with Julie Christie and one or two others. The ambassador made a very good speech about the determination of the Chilean government to pursue justice. All I can tell you is that *Moonlight* opened this week and *Oleanna* comes back next week, but this visit to the Embassy seemed to me of the first importance. I think it's absolutely essential that these matters never be forgotten.

MG: You still are as politically active as you have been in recent years?

HP: Yes. Absolutely. That's what I'm saying. I was also thinking about something else you raised yesterday, the discussion of the political plays and *Moonlight*. You said you felt there was something very personal about *Moonlight* as opposed to the others. I know how you

120

were using the word 'personal'. There's a distinction to be made about what I actually think and what is expressed in the plays. My awareness of the facts of torture and states of affairs that exist in the world I take very personally indeed.

First, I've met people who have been tortured, in Turkey. Secondly, I've read a lot of stuff about the whole matter, including a remarkable book called *Nunca Mas*. There was an official government commission in Argentina after the dictatorship folded. Alfonsin, the president, came in and set up an official commission into the facts. And the facts were so *harrowing*, so utterly utterly dreadful that they really have to be read. Whether anybody can express that in a play is another question altogether. I know the last line in my play *One for the Road* people still find very shocking. The last exchange, when the victim is being led out: the father says, how is my son? He says, oh your son, don't worry about him, he was a little prick. That was the last line. When they were arresting his mother and father, the little boy kicked the soldier.

MG: What stirs you to take a stand?

HP: I want to be as objective and as lucid about this as possible. My own view is that the world situation has actually changed for the worse, including the fact that the United States now has no constraint upon it and is able to act with only the very slightest reference to anybody else. I think this is a very dangerous situation. Even as we sit here, last night in Somalia, U.S. helicopters, under the umbrella of the United Nations, killed over a hundred Somali women and children, who the U.S. forces said were threatening them and their colleagues. That's another 100 Somalian people gone down the drain. The United Nations was supposed to be bringing humanitarian aid. They were supposed to be bringing food and water. What's actually happened is

that the United States is more or less running riot. I
know the whole cliché of the Wild West, but it does
hit one.

I want to make one other small point, then sum this up.
A few weeks ago the U.S. sent missiles on Baghdad
because they said Bush's life had been threatened
last year. This was blatantly a move on Clinton's part to
say, look, I can do this too. We have a great friend here,
who's a Syrian woman, Rana Kabbani. She's a writer.
One of her great friends was an Iraqi artist, called
Leila al-Attar. She also ran a museum. She's dead.
Those missiles killed her and her husband, and members
of her family. The next morning Clinton was on his way
to church. Asked how he felt about the missile attack, he
said, 'I feel good about it, and I'm sure the American
people will feel good about it as well.' Well, that's
great! I'm very happy that he feels good, and the
American people are going to feel good, according to
him. That woman is dead, and there are plenty of others.
This kind of action represents a terrible doublethink. The
word 'punish' is used; that isn't doublethink, it's quite
direct. But claims for freedom and democracy are
thrown around all over the place – and don't forget
'Christian values', too. I'm very surprised by the lack of
criticism of United States foreign policy in the United
States press. I'm surprised there isn't a much more
rigorous scrutiny. Death has been degutted.

MG: Almost decriminalized.

HP: Yes. Remember that film, *A Walk in the Sun*, many
years ago, the great Richard Conte walking around in
Italy saying, 'Nobody dies, nobody dies.' There's a
tremendous schism between the reality of death and how
we're educated to look at it.

MG: Can we talk about the role of art in politics?

HP: Theatre is essentially exploratory. Even old Sophocles didn't know what was going to happen next. He had to find his way through unknown territory. At the same time, theatre has always been a critical act, looking in a broad sense at the society in which we live and attempting to reflect and dramatize these findings. We're not talking about the moon.

These are excavations. As a writer, you're subjecting yourself and the society in which you live, and the world in which you live, to a critical scrutiny. You don't have to do it baldly. James Joyce, for example, in *Ulysses* is not making critical judgments about anyone; he's setting down truths, which implicitly contain a certain kind of irony. There's criticism involved in the ironic stance. I think a lot of art does possess that ironic touch.

MG: As a playwright, you think of yourself as an explorer?

HP: I certainly do.

MG: You write to find out what you think?

HP: I don't set out with such intention, but I find at the end of the journey, which of course is never ending, that I have found things out. I don't make any great claims for all that. I don't go away and say, 'I have *illuminated* myself. You see before you a changed person.' [He smiles.] It's a more surreptitious sense of discovery that happens to the writer himself.

MG: What did you discover in writing *Moonlight*?'

HP: I think I said yesterday that I found a sense of how the dead were present. I think there is another aspect in *Moonlight*, which I didn't know about when I started to write it. I didn't think about it. This is a tentative attempt at understanding, by no means a definitive statement.

It's simply that Andy says at one point that he doesn't know what death is. It's a question of the horizon. He doesn't know how light it is, how dark it is, anything. He doesn't know what the attributes of death are. But all this time Bridget is walking around in his life. As a ghost, she is present in his life. But he can't define her. He can't hold her.

It does strike me, though, that in our conversation about *Moonlight* there is possibly an unbalanced emphasis on death. Though we know there's a lot of death about in *Moonlight*, salt, vinegar and mustard exist in the play. In other words there are a few laughs. That may have to do with death, but it also has to do with life.

MG: During this 15-year period since *Betrayal,* were there false starts at plays?

HP: Yes, yes. Bumped into a brick wall on all occasions. I can tell very quickly when there's a real juice going, and it hasn't happened. There were a lot of false starts. Sometimes, the image, like the ghost, begins to pale away, doesn't have the same strength and resonance that it seemed to have at the time. It has even less as the years go on. You'll be happy to hear I still exercise a lot of critical judgement. A number of things I've said to myself I'd like to write, and I've scribbled a few lines. I give it a couple of days or so, and I realize it's really no good.

MG: It seems clear that there's an intellectual direction to the work, as it's being written.

HP: I'm well aware that my work is packed with literary references. Of course I am. I know what they are too. [Laughs.] I'm writing away and in the act of that writing, these references occur. It happens very quickly: a kind of intuition is involved. At the same time, I know intellectually what's going on. In *Moonlight*, two lines come to mind, with the boys, 'gemless in Wall Street to the bank with fuck all.' Now that is my little slant on 'Eyeless in Gaza, to the mill with slaves.' *Samson Agonistes*.

MG: On the other hand, it's always interesting to see academics over-reading your plays. Did you see that structuralist reading of your revue sketch, *Last to Go*?

HP: I couldn't believe it.

MG: [Reading.] '*Last to Go* presents a conversation that is mutually and simultaneously phatic for both interlocutors, maintaining contact but not conveying much information between them . . . Utterances that in a non-aesthetic context might be classified as dominantly reverential, emotive, conative, etc. acquire a different status when they occur in an aesthetic context. Language that is phatic for the Barman and the Newspaper-seller is poetic for us . . . The semiotic structure of the sketch might therefore be summarized as: Speech is to Silence as George is to the last newspaper to go.'

HP: I don't understand how people can be so terribly earnest and serious about this damned sketch. It's only a sketch.

MG: I was looking back at our first conversation more than 20 years ago. You said, 'I think I am in a trap always. I sometimes wish desperately that I could write like someone else, *be* someone else.' You no longer feel that way, do you?

HP: No. [Laughs.] I think I've settled to be *myself*, and write like myself.

MG: Are you happy with yourself?

HP: I'm actually much happier *in* myself than I was 20 years ago.

MG: What do you think you were like 20 years ago?

HP: [Pause.] The fact is I re-read that interview too the other day. And apart from anything else, one thing struck me. When I talked about the closeness of my family, I was in fact very unhappy. I was, I suppose, protecting my privacy. But it was not true. I was not happy, and I had not been happy for some time.

MG: Do you want to talk about your first wife? She remains one of the best interpreters of your early work.

HP: Yes, she was a wonderfully talented actress.

MG: You were actors together.

HP: Yes, and when we were actors together we were very happy. That was in the very early days. We were terribly terribly poor too, when our son was born. I mean *really* poor, and even poorer after *The Birthday Party* came on and off in 1958. We were both about 28. At one point, I did my accounts and I said, 'Don't worry, we still have 60 pounds.' I remember it very clearly. I said, 'By the end of this month, we will still have 60 pounds.' When you're right against the wire, you share a lot. We both in fact fought our way out of it. She was pretty indomitable in those days. She was acting with a three month old baby in the dressing room. She used to feed him in the intervals. I was in and out of work myself. I did a bit of acting. I was incredibly thin in those days, mainly because there was very little to eat. [Laughs.]

MG: Did you think about getting a job?

HP: You mean a Real Job? I did one day's work in an office, in 1958, a factory office. I had to. I don't know if you know a sketch of mine called *Trouble in the Works*. I got that from the office. That was quite a fruitful day. I was supposed to be a clerk. I had to make a list of all these machine part tools. I suddenly came across these names. I couldn't believe it. I thought a bit of French Surrealism had crept in to this factory in Brentford, or wherever it was. I made a note of all these names. High speed taper shank spiral flute reamers, and a magnificent one, a jaw for Jacob's chuck for use on portable drill. I did one day, and at the end of the day the head of the department came to me – I got my temporary two cents, or whatever it was – he looked at what I had been doing. It didn't take all that much wit to file things beginning with an A under A, and B under B. He said, 'Have you thought about taking this up as a career?' I said, 'Well, no, I actually hadn't.' He said, 'If you ever want a job, come back, there'll be one here.' I never went back.

MG: And from that day came a sketch. It was a profitable day.

HP: Yes, it was. So, anyway, under those trying circumstances, we were a very close-knit family. But that was way back.

MG: Then things changed as you both became more successful?

HP: Yes. I think in a way Vivien probably enjoyed acting in rep more than anything else. There was less pressure, naturally. We were in Torquay, Bournemouth, those places. You worked very hard, but we were young and we could take it. But gradually, as the big world started to roll up, I think it proved rather destructive. It wasn't the world, but we couldn't deal with it. I think I dealt with it slightly better than she did. Listen, Vivien was a hell of an actress and a woman of undoubted independence of mind. She had a really independent mind, but having said that, she was also very dependent.

MG: Was she closely involved in your work?

HP: No.

MG: Just to play the roles.

HP: Well, she always read the plays. She did enjoy what I wrote. And she did give some wonderful performances.

MG: Certainly her Ruth [in *The Homecoming*] stands out.

HP: Oh yes. There's never quite been a Ruth like Vivien.

MG: Arthur Miller once said to me, speaking for himself and for Tennessee Williams, 'Redemption lies in writing. That's when you're most alive, at your most intense functioning.' That almost sounds religious. Does that ring a note with you?

HP: You're redeemed through the act of writing? Well I wouldn't know. I couldn't possibly use such a term. But I would certainly say that writing for me is an act of freedom and celebration. Whatever I'm writing about, it's a celebration. What you're celebrating is the ability to write. There's an excitement about it that certainly transcends whatever you might have been doing five minutes before. It takes you way out into another country.

MG: I think what Miller meant was it justified his . . .

HP: . . . existence. My life is an odd one. When I was about 13, and back in London during the war, with my mother and father, we woke up one night. There was an air raid alarm. We opened the back door of the house where there was a little garden. It was entirely in flames, the whole garden, and all the gardens along. They had dropped incendiary bombs. So we had to evacuate the house immediately. I took two things with me, a cricket bat, and a bit of writing.

MG: What were you writing?

HP: I was in love at the time. I was somewhat precocious and desperately in love with a girl down the street. I think I was writing some paean of love. I think it was a prose poem. You'll be happy to know I've lost it.

MG: Those were the two most meaningful things to you at the time.

HP: Yes. I was born with a cricket bat. I'm not telling you I was a great cricketer. But sport always meant a lot to me, and writing, and of course love. In a sense, I hardly know when I didn't write. As soon as I hit adolescence, that was it.

MG: You've also said that running was very important to you.

HP: I was very fast. I broke two sprint records in school, in 1946, 100 and 220 yards. I did it both one afternoon. It's in the school magazine. They've been broken since. They were pretty fast. It was pure brute force, no style at all. I loved sport. I still do.

MG: You don't run anymore?

HP: No. I run on the tennis court. I still move about.

MG: What is it about place names that interest you? And names of flowers. Some academic will do a thesis on the uses of hibiscus and jacaranda in the plays of Harold Pinter. Do you like the sound of these words?

HP: I do! When Antonia and I got together, she came to see *A Slight Ache*. At the very beginning the wife says to the husband, 'Have you seen the clematis recently, and the japonica.' Antonia said to me, 'And what does the japonica look like?' I said I haven't the faintest idea. [Hearty laugh.]

129

MG: There is a re-occurrence of certain names.

HP: We all have our mysterious preoccupations.

MG: And what about Balls Pond Road? That appears in an earlier play and then in *Moonlight*. It actually exists, around Islington.

HP: Well, Balls Pond Road is very near where I was born. It's a very famous road. Dalston Junction. Balls Pond Road. I suppose there must have been a Balls Pond there once, back in the 16th century.

MG: What about the names the boys say in *Moonlight*? Are they real people?

HP: No, no. They're just names.

MG: Do you have right-wing friends?

HP: I must have one or two, I suppose, because there are so few left-wing people about. I don't ask people their credentials. There's been a change in one or two other friends over the years. It's not that they've become more left wing, whatever that is, but they're become more critical, more questioning, less tied in to received ideas. I know I've had the reputation of being a real pain in the arse over the last few years and on certain occasions I really have been a pain in the arse. I wouldn't deny it. It made life extremely uncomfortable, not only for others but for myself too.

People who stand on a spurious sense of dignity do irritate the shit out of me. The solemnity of the official position! Essentially to cover up murderous activities. East Timor, for example. The complicity of your country and my country. Indonesia is an appalling authoritarian state, which has actually killed hundreds of thousands of people in East Timor. The U.S. Congress is on the point of passing a bill which says that no more arms will be sold to Indonesia unless they do very serious things about their human rights record. I'm very pleased to see the U.S. Congress has done this, but it's 25 years too late. Perhaps it's never too late, but if they had done that 25 years ago, those 200,000 people wouldn't have died. And *Great* Britain still sells arms to everyone in sight, and certainly to Indonesia. And then there's the whole Iraq stuff, and all that corruption and masquerade. [Pause.] I wouldn't make a good politician. [Laughs.]

MG: Have you ever come to blows with anyone?

HP: It's quite an old story. Many years ago, in the 60's, I came to blows with a fellow. I was in a bar, and I heard a man talking about Hitler and the Jews, saying that Hitler hadn't gone far enough. He was a very respectably dressed man. I always remember his suit, tie, so on. I suddenly heard myself say, 'Stop talking such shit,' or something like that. He said to me, 'I suppose you're a filthy Yid yourself.' And I said, 'Say that again,' and he did say it again. So I hit him. I've always remembered this spurt of blood on his cheek. I can see it. He went right back against the bar, and I picked up my drink and started to give him a little sermon on what not to say, and suddenly he hit me when I was still holding my glass. Thereupon all hell broke loose. I went at him quite wildly. The whole thing was chaos. The police came. I was taken to the railway office. There was a witness. This fellow said I'm going to charge you for assault. The witness then said, 'He insulted this man.' He insulted me. He told the policeman what he said. So far as I was concerned, he wasn't insulting me, he was insulting a whole lot of other people. The policeman said to the guy, 'If I were you, I'd drop the whole thing and don't cause a public nuisance of yourself.'

Then this man came over to me. He had blood on his white shirt. He said, 'I don't know what I'm going to say to my wife.' I shrugged, and he said, 'I want to ask you a question. Are you a Jew?' I said, 'Yes.' He said, 'Ah, well, I can understand why you hit me, but why did you hit me so hard?' I couldn't answer that question. I knew the answer, because he had insulted so many people with that one statement.

I haven't had any physical violence since then, though there have been close shaves. There is a violence in me, but I don't walk about the street looking for trouble.

MG: How do you feel about critics?

HP: I wouldn't say I feel particularly *warmly* towards critics, but neither do I feel any real hostility or antagonism towards critics who undoubtedly feel that about me.

MG: How did you feel about Kenneth Tynan? In the earliest days, he was very dismissive of both you and Beckett.

HP: I'll tell you something Tynan said to me. In 1958, with *The Birthday Party*, there was an absolute massacre. Then someone heard that Hobson [in the Sunday Times] was going to be good. What we needed was that Tynan [in the Observer] would perhaps save the play. Someone did speak to him, and he said he was not very enthusiastic about it. On the Sunday, he actually said there have been plays about this before – the artist in society, the artist as poor victim – and he dismissed it on those grounds, that it was a play about an artist in society, and who cares about that? So the play closed. About four or five years later, I found myself with him on a television programme about Donald Wolfit. I had acted in his company and Tynan had written about him. I was naturally civil.

MG: *Naturally* civil?

HP: I'm a naturally civil person. What I didn't say to him was, are you the Tynan who didn't like my play? We had a drink in the pub next door. We drank for about an hour. Then he said the following to me: 'You know, I really enjoyed this drink. If only I had known you were such a pleasant guy, I might have written a different notice of *The Birthday Party*.' It was a devastating thing to hear.

MG: Compared to most American playwrights, you would seem to have had a fair run of criticism.

HP: Yes and no. I'm not prepared to complain about anything in that area. Some people don't like my work, and some do. Some people like some particular plays better than others.

MG: And after the fact, they change their opinions. They decide they like the earlier plays better, and ask, why doesn't he write political plays as he used to?

HP: That's right.

MG: I was curious about some of your directing choices. Why did you choose to direct *Vanilla*?

HP: It's not an entirely achieved satire, but I think it's much sharper and much funnier than was appreciated here. It was totally dismissed here. I believe it had a lot to do with me. They treated it badly because I was involved. I did it because I thought it was great fun.

MG: I didn't think so. I thought it was a case that you directed it for the money.

HP: Let me tell you, you never direct for the money. It's a very arduous bloody thing, directing, and there's no guarantee you're going to get anything out of it. I thought it was a real satire on riches. I don't think it was exaggerated.

MG: Was there a play you regretted directing?

HP: Yes, I shouldn't have directed the last play of Simon Gray's I directed, *The Common Pursuit*. I was very unhappy directing that, and I had just given up smoking, too. It was an absolute disaster. Simon's written this book about it, which is quite funny I have to say and pretty accurate. It was not a good experience, but I had such marvellous experiences with his other plays. Except for one other play of his which wasn't anyone's fault, *Close of Play*, at the National. Peggy Ashcroft was going to be in it. She started rehearsing, and she was going to be quite wonderful, but she had this operation on her knee and had to leave the production. She would have brought the whole thing together. Pretty good cast there too, Michael Redgrave, Michael Gambon, Anna Massey. Apart from that . . . [Pause] *Sweet Bird of Youth* [with Lauren Bacall] was hard work. Although she was great. It's an unwieldy piece. The play I really had a tremendous time with as Donald Freed's *Circe and Bravo*. I thought it was really an original piece of work.

MG: I thought it was marginally better than *Vanilla*. [Pinter laughs loudly.] You're not going to direct Simon Gray again?

HP: No, no, no.

MG: But you are still friends.

HP: Yes. We're very very close friends, very much so.

MG: Every one of your screenplays has been an adaptation. Haven't you been tempted to write an original?

HP: No. I've never had the impulse.

MG: It's been a different author each time. How do you choose your films?

HP: They're almost invariably offered to me. Ironically, the only one that wasn't offered to me was *Remains of the Day*. I read the book in proof and bought an option. Then it became a best seller. There were a number of inquiries which I didn't want to pursue. Then Mike Nichols suddenly called and said I just read this book and tried to find out who had the film rights and it turned out to be you. I said that's right. He and I worked together. I did a screenplay. Mike simply couldn't get a budget that would suit him. It started to wobble. Suddenly, Ivory-Merchant came into it, wanted to do it, and that all went immediately like that [snaps fingers] because *Howard's End* had been a big success. Tony Hopkins was already in it. I met Ivory and Merchant once and they didn't really discuss the screenplay, which they'd read, obviously. We talked about locations and actors, and we parted, and I never heard another word. I got one letter about three or four months later. They just went to Ruth Prawer Jhabvala,who wrote them a totally new screenplay, which they're doing. There's one thing for the record. Merchant has been saying one thing: that I approve and I'm a part of it. It's not so. I've withdrawn my name from the film.

MG: Did they want to credit the screenplay to the two of you?

HP: Yes. But I wouldn't. I've never done that in my life. It's her screenplay though they have used a number of my scenes.

MG: Your Losey films stand up.

HP: Oh, I think so too. *The Servant*, *Accident* and *The Go-Between* – and *Proust*. I worked with him a great deal and still miss him. That was a really rich working relationship, and I was very fond of him . . .

I don't regard *The Trial* as a particularly political work. I think bureaucracy figures very strongly in it, obviously. There's a very deep religious conundrum in it. A lot of people think that Kafka was writing about Communism. He actually wrote the book before the Russian revolution. His reference of course was the Austro-Hungarian empire. Prague, which we see in the film, has those great pillars, the bank, a very strong solid world indeed, with a worm of anxiety in the very middle of it. Looking back, or rather, looking forward, you can see elements where a society in a very surreptitious and appalling way is grinding you into the dust.

MG: Kafka's on your list with Joyce, Proust and Dostoevski.

HP: Oh, yes. Definitely. I'd like to have had a drink with Kafka, too.

MG: Do you feel that strongly about any of your contemporaries – novelists and poets as well as playwrights?

HP: There are one or two poets that mean a lot to me, a Scottish poet called W. S. Graham whom I think is wonderful. George Barker, a remarkable man and poet. George Barker, who died last year in his 80's, was a really mischievous old bugger. You know I publish a bit of poetry. I was opening this launching and said a few words. George Barker took a chair and sat right in front of me. I said things like, all we have left is the English language. After I stopped, there was a moment of silence and George Barker said, 'You don't really believe all that shit, do you?' [Laughs.] The great thing was, I did, and so did he. He knew that I knew, etc.

I recently discovered a wonderful Scots poet, called

Tom Scott. An elderly man, again. He's a major force, I think. He writes in the Scots dialect and his work is informed by a real indignation. He's in a towering splenetic rage most the time.

MG: What novelists?

HP: I don't read many modern novels. I do find my reading goes back to Nazi Germany. I read a lot about Nazi Germany. At the moment I'm reading a biography of Heidegger. It's not my field, but I take an interest. Before that, I read a biography of Wittgenstein, which just came out. Heidegger became a Nazi apologist. He was a Nazi. I think the whole period is probably the worst thing that ever happened.

MG: *Reunion* is the only time you've dealt even indirectly with the Holocaust?

HP: Yes.

MG: Would you ever write about it?

HP [pause]: I don't know. There's something in me that wants to do something about it. It's so difficult.

MG: Do you go to the movies often?

HP: Not often . . . You know American movies meant an awful lot to me. I was brought up on them. I had a very rich cinematic education, much more than the theatre. I never went to the theatre.

MG: What movies did you see?

HP: I'm talking about the 1940's. I saw all the American black and white gangster films, which were great.

MG: Bogart, Cagney, Robinson?

HP: Oh, yeah. I didn't miss one. And later William Bendix, Alan Ladd, Brian Donlevy. *The Glass Key*. All those B films. Franchot Tone, Elisha Cook, Jr. I saw *The Ox-Bow Incident* and *The Grapes of Wrath*, John Ford. Then *The Long Voyage Home*, which left a great impression on me. At the same time, at the age of 14, I joined the local film club, and I ran right into Eisenstein and Pudovkin and Dovzhenko, *The Cabinet of Dr. Caligari* – and Buñuel and Cocteau. I saw *L'Age d'Or* and *Chien Andalou* when I was 14. That was my language, apart from reading. The theatre didn't really come into it until much later.

MG: Have films been an influence on your work? Buñuel on *Party Time*?

HP: I suppose I never ask myself that. The American thrillers, there was something to do with the language then, very sharp, very terse [snaps fingers] and Hemingwayish. I was reading Hemingway at the time.

MG: It was the American not the British movies.

HP: I omitted one other element, the British war films. I don't know if you ever saw *The Way Ahead*. It was a great British war film, with David Niven, Carol Reed directed it, and Peter Ustinov wrote the script. Vivien [Merchant] was in it. She was nine. She played Stanley Holloway's daughter. He came back from the war. There's a scene where she's nine years old and playing the radio. She was a funny looking little girl. It was a nice little scene. She would always tell the story that she was taken by her mother, and she was called back and called back and she finally got the part. She said to herself, I must be the prettiest girl here. Actually quite the opposite was the case. But it was a damned good film. And the French cinema. Carné. Duvivier. *Carnet du Bal*. I even saw *Que viva Mexico*.

MG: Did this make you want to be an actor, or a writer?

HP: Just as a plain old moviegoer.

MG: Any favourite among the actors?

HP: I fell in love quite a lot in those days, people like Veronica Parker. I was crazy about Gene Tierney. Lana Turner. And an English actress called Patricia Roc. It was a long time ago. I was also in on *The Naked City*, Jules Dassin. I thought *The Ox-Bow Incident* was a great film. William Wellman, Henry Fonda, a young Anthony Quinn, and Dana Andrews. I was very pleased when we did *The Last Tycoon* many many years later, we had a hell of a cast list. De Niro and Robert Mitchum and also Dana Andrews, Ray Milland and John Carradine!

In Pinter's study, there is a shelf of scrapbooks of his cuttings (or clippings) which he has been saving since his career began. On the first page of the first volume is The Room, *his first play, in March 1957. 'Written in Two Days. This Young Author Scores a Hit' reads the headline in a Bristol newspaper. The review praises his 'rare vitality' and says, 'with experience and greater conciseness,' Mr. Pinter 'may well make some impact as a playwright.' But soon in other reviews there are comments like 'Mr. Pinter, you're just not funny enough' and 'What all this means only Mr. Pinter knows.' There are all the negative reviews of* The Birthday Party, *followed by Hobson's rescuing notice – then, the programme for the Scarborough production, with Ayckbourn as Stanley and Pinter directing. As we leaf through them, I ask why he has kept the clippings. He says, 'I just started doing it and it became a habit.'*

MG: You've kept the bad notices and articles along with the good ones. Actors often say they don't read notices.

HP: I always have. In those days, I didn't have the papers delivered. I used to go out and buy a newspaper when I could afford it.

MG: Before *The Birthday Party* opened, did you think it would receive good reviews?

HP: Yes. I was totally unrealistic.

MG: If Hobson had not come along with his notice, might you have been discouraged from writing more plays?

HP: I felt pretty discouraged *before* Hobson. He had a tremendous influence on my life.

MG: Peggy Ramsay told me that she prodded Hobson to see the play, despite the fact that it was closing. Hobson sent me a letter verifying that he went at Peggy's urging.

HP: I never knew that.

MG: I would say that was a true turning point in your life.

HP: Well, as I say, that had a direct bearing, because I was thinking of saying, what the hell, I'll just go back to writing novels. I had written my novel by this time.

MG: Had you tried to publish it?

HP: No, I didn't think there was much point.

MG: Even though you wrote from an early age, did you ever think that you would be a writer, could be a writer?

HP: No. I was writing poems, a few of which were published, and you can't earn a living by publishing a few poems. I knew I would continue to write something or other. But playwriting was obviously a disaster, so I was quite prepared to continue to earn a kind of living as an actor. Then my old friend Pat Magee was working a lot with the BBC, doing Beckett with Donald McWhinnie. He introduced me to Donald McWhinnie, and he commissioned me to write a play for radio. *A Slight Ache*. I had nothing, 60 pounds, and the BBC paid 60 pounds for the commission. So suddenly I was rich.

MG: If there were no Hobson, and you had decided to make a living as an actor, where would it have led you?

HP: I think I had the capability of being a reasonably

intelligent actor. As you know, I recently came back and did *No Man's Land*. Quite daunting. The whole damn world looking at you and waiting for you to fall on your arse.

What would have happened? I think I would have probably gone into direction. When I went to join McMaster, I was aware of the sense and shape of the event, the narrative.

MG: Was University not a possibility?

HP: In those days, 1948, the only universities you wanted to go to were Oxford and Cambridge. Those were the attractive ones, but you needed Latin. My Latin was non-existent. I took one week of Latin. That's where I picked up the term 'periphrastic conjugation'. I remember saying to my friend Henry Woolf, who later directed *The Room*, 'Listen, Woolf, you're nothing but a periphrastic conjugation.' I took French and Spanish. I wasn't terribly interested in learning. I actually wanted to be an actor. I did act at school, played Macbeth and Romeo. And I wanted to get out in the world. But I was also a conscientious objector, so that complicated it as well.

MG: Any regrets?

HP: No. It seems to be a rich life. If Hobson had not written that review, I think I would have remained in the theatre. The theatre was my world. It was the only world I was happy in. In fact, shortly afterwards, when Donald McWhinnie commissioned a play, he just said here's some money, go and write a play. He didn't say, send in a synopsis, send in a treatment. He said, go and write a play. *A Slight Ache,* which is a play which I'm particularly attached to, was just waiting around the corner. I didn't know it was there. It spilled out. It was all waiting. I'm sure it would have come out later.

MG: When you work, do you work mornings?

HP: No, no, no. Absolutely not. A great deal of my life is administration. I have an enormous correspondence. I have a secretary who's very busy. There's any amount of telephone calls. I have an agent who's very busy. There's always a lot going on all over the world, which comes in. My plays being done. Next year, for example, is going to be busier.

Moonlight is suddenly going all over the place. Amsterdam and Berlin in April, Dublin, Prague, Mexico City, and then later in Paris. Meanwhile there's a production of *The Homecoming* in Paris, which I'm interested in. I'm going to Stockholm to see *The Homecoming* next month at the Royal National Theatre, directed by Thommy Berggren. I've never been to Stockholm. I like arriving places. It's the getting there I don't like. I've seen two productions of *Party Time*, one with *One for the Road* in Amsterdam and Zurich last year. I went to Prague and saw *Mountain Language*. If I wanted to, I could just keep moving all the time.

In China there's an extraordinarily successful production of *The Lover*, of all things. The theatre in Shanghai is at this moment touring *The Lover* throughout China. Jung Chang happened to be in China this year and saw it. They've hardly done western plays in China. Arthur Miller has done his own. And one or two others. *The Lover*, being a play about sex in the English suburbs, strikes me as really rum. I think they set it in the Hong Kong suburbs. Apart from China, they are done everywhere. It's all part of the tapestry of my working life. I don't arrange the productions, but sometimes I have to give my permission for particular productions.

MG: What's the range of letters and requests?

HP: There is a considerable amount of letters from

students from all over, studying plays, not just in England. I also get letters on all manner of political issues, since I've declared myself an interested person. All these issues are worthy, but not all can be dealt with. I'm just one man here. A lot of them ask for money. Sometimes I'm able to help them in a limited way. This chap, Vanunu, in Israel, he's in solitary confinement for over eight years. I'm a member of the Trust. We don't leave the Israeli government alone on this. We think his sentence was deplorable, and the solitary confinement extremely harsh. He was given 18 years for telling the world what the world knew already, that Israel had a nuclear capacity. In a couple of weeks there's a big concert, an evening which I'm taking part in, at Hackney Empire, where I used to go as a child. There's a whole range of things.

MG [indicating a stack of papers on a shelf]: All those things over here?

HP: Yes. International PEN. Human Rights in Northern Ireland. Israel. Liberty. Kurds in Turkey. Amnesty. The Medical Foundation for the Victims of Torture. Then of course, there's Guatemala and Nicaragua. And I'm often asked to make statements. And East Timor. I keep a lot of cuttings on all these things.

MG: When I visited Beckett in the nursing home, he had only two books with him, a dictionary and his schoolboy copy of *The Divine Comedy*.

HP: I visited him in that nursing home, too. That's when I had my last conversation with him. I said, 'How are you feeling, really?' He said, 'Oh, not so good, pretty gloomy.' And I said, 'Look, I'm going to send you something, which is really going to cheer you up. My adaptation of Kafka's *The Trial*.' He guffawed. The thing was he was reading it when he died. So I'll never know what he thought.

MG: Where does your son live and what is he doing?

HP: He lives alone in the country, he writes music and we're in touch.

MG: Did you have any problems with your father?

HP: No, I didn't. We had plenty of tensions at an early stage. He says a wonderful thing now when I call him. He's getting on to 92. I say, 'How are things, Dad?' He says, 'Well, no fireworks.'

MG: He's waiting for the fireworks?

HP: He seems to imply the fireworks have not yet arrived.

MG: As if to say, when were the good times?

HP: And when will they come again . . .

MG: Any movies coming up?

HP: Not at the moment. [Pause.] I have a certain sense that the kind of way I worked in movies over all these years is narrowing. I suppose I take this from the experience with *Remains of the Day*: writing a script and then the director getting someone else to write a script. That never happened to me over all this time. My position is: I've always written a screenplay, and that's the screenplay that's been done. The only exception, slightly, was *The Handmaid's Tale*, which I stopped writing, I was exhausted. I told Volker Schlöndorff to go and get Margaret Atwood to do whatever. What he really did was to get the actors to write a lot of it, although there's still a lot of my stuff in it. That was a bit of a stew, but there was enough of me to still keep my name on it. *Remains of the Day*, as I told you, is a totally different story.

MG: Did you get paid for *Remains of the Day*?

HP: Oh, yes. I did indeed. I had my contractual rights, clear and concrete. Nevertheless, payment or no payment, it's a disappointment. I worked quite a long time at it. But it's all over. I'm not crying about it. I simply never found myself in that tradition, the tradition of many writers being brought in to a film. The classic Hollywood tradition.

MG: Will you do fewer screenplays or start more projects yourself?

HP: I think that will probably be the thing. But I really still do find film a fascinating craft. It's rather nice for a change to be flexible and on your toes. I have no actual plans, which is great. It's been a hell of a busy year.

MG: What are you doing next?

HP [laughing]: I think I'll take a break.

MG: Tell me about directors. Could you compare Peter Hall, David Leveaux, David Jones, yourself?

HP: [Pause.] Listen. In a way, what you're really asking for is a book. Those three and me, make it four, have one thing in common, which is absolute concentration on the text. Those three have a real sense of language and the shape of language, on stage.

MG: Not all directors do?

HP: No, not all directors do. I have the highest regard for all three. I worked with each a number of times. Peter, as you know, did *The Homecoming* again about two years ago. I was very pleased.

MG: You would work with Peter Hall again?

HP: Definitely. We had a brief unfortunate kind of hiatus, which I'm happy is all over. These things happen.

MG: More in the theatre than anywhere else?

HP: I don't know, since I know no other world. Don't they happen in what's called business?

MG: You've worked on three sides of the profession, as an actor, director and writer; it's a volatile profession.

HP: Volatility has not been the operation.

MG: Do you like actors?

HP: Of course I do, I love actors. I understand actors. I'm an actor myself. My intention is to be helpful as a director, guide things along, find out what's going on, that's what a director should be doing.

MG: Some directors manipulate actors to get what result they want.

HP: I once knew a producer. I will not name names. We were doing a play, and I was directing it. A friend of mine was the author, and another friend was the leading actor. We all went to see the producer: why wasn't he advertising the show more? He said, 'I don't believe in advertising, I don't think it does any good at all. I'm not prepared to do it.' I said, 'Look, OK, it would be very fruitful if you came down to theatre, we'll get the actors together and you can explain why you've come to this conclusion.' He said, 'You want me to *talk* to a load of actors?' The leading actor was sitting there. We were flabbergasted. We dropped the whole thing, went out and got drunk. [Laughs.] He couldn't *believe* he was being seriously asked to explain himself to actors.

We were doing *The Go-Between*, the film, years ago

with Joe Losey. Julie Christie was playing the daughter. We hadn't got the money and Joe Losey said, 'You know who would be wonderful? If we could get Anne Bancroft for the mother, then we'd have the money.' She had already done *The Pumpkin Eater*. She could do English. He said, 'You know Anne Bancroft, call her.' So I said, 'OK.' I called her and said, 'Anne, it's Harold here.' 'Harold! Hello, how are you?' This is across the Atlantic. I said, 'We're doing this movie, *The Go-Between*. Joseph Losey.' She said, 'Joe. Of course.' 'It's all Edwardian and it has aristocrats and a farmer and a daughter and a mother and she suspects the daughter is having an affair with the farmer, etc., etc., and it all takes place in this beautiful weather, and we'd love you to play the mother.' And she said, 'It sounds terrific.' 'Are you free?' 'I'm absolutely free. Tell me one thing, who is playing the daughter?' I said, 'Julie Christie.' There's this great pause across the Atlantic and she said, 'You want me to play Julie Christie's *mother*?'

MG: Acting is such a vulnerable profession.

HP: On these two productions[*Moonlight* and *Oleanna*], one of which I did myself, I got more and more to appreciate what's demanded of actors. And Ian's [Holm] courage in coming back here after that layoff. I remember too Lia Williams in *Oleanna*. The first night, when David Suchet beat her up, the men in the audience really gave her a rough time, and cheered. She wasn't expecting it. We were told it wasn't going to happen in England. Not every night, but it happens. She was very thrown by it, deeply distressed, and thought they didn't like her. I had to say to her, it's not you. The only thing you can do is stand up for yourself and say I'm above all this, as the character does. She's indomitable, whether you like her or not. She can say, you've beaten me up, I'm hurt, but nevertheless you're going to make this statement. When that happens in our last five minutes, the audience is absolutely silent. Lia has really triumphed too. It's not very pleasant to be detested on stage, to find the audience antagonistic. But I think she's won tremendous respect.

MG: You've said that at a very early age you came to dislike audiences.

HP: My closest friends laugh at this. The actors do, too. As a director I give the actors one note at the very end of the other notes, one note: fuck the audience. And every actor knows what I'm talking about. If you want the audience to love you, you're finished! When an audience is a good and intelligent audience I like them as well as anybody does. But you've got to take a very strong view, saying you're going to get what we're giving you, you're not going to get what you want. There has to be someone in charge of a theatrical enterprise, and it *has* to be the work itself.

MG: In your speech in Bristol in 1962, you said, 'What I write has no obligation to anything other than itself . . . not to audience, critics, producers, directors, actors or to my fellow men in general, but to the play in hand.' That was 31 years ago. Do you still hold to that?

HP: I do. I haven't changed a bit really. [Laughs.] No, I *absolutely* hold to that . . .

MG: You've not written real introductions, just used speeches and statements. You never want to explain your work.

HP: If the work can stand on its feet, which it does, then it's much more interesting. I do *talk* about the work. That's one of the things we have been doing. But I don't know how fruitful what an author says about his own work can be. If you're talking about the theatre, what happens on the stage is it! That's all that needs to be said. That's why it's such a delicate enterprise in the

149

first place. All the component parts that have to come together, to be integrated: the actors, director, the design, the words, the lighting [snaps his fingers], the whole structure of the event. When it all comes together, it's thrilling.

B*efore Pinter held a rehearsal of* Oleanna *at the Duke of York's, we met for lunch near the theatre.*

MG: It could be said that in the early 1980s, about 1983 or 1984, there was a down point in your work.

HP: There was a down time, yes.

MG: What were you doing in terms of the plays?

HP: In terms of the plays? I was not writing.

MG: Between *A Kind of Alaska* and *One for the Road.*

HP: There was a period of roughly three years when I did not write a play. Something gnaws away – the desire to write something and the inability to do so. But you have to accept it. I'm not the kind of writer who can force anything. It's impossible. I cannot force a word out if it's not there to come out. I think I was getting more and more imbedded in international issues. The last play I had done was *A Kind of Alaska*, inspired by Oliver Sacks, about a woman who had been asleep for 29 years and wakes up. It was very important for me to explore this thing. Then I wrote *Family Voices*, about a family, a very short, 45-minute play but packed with incident. Then *Victoria Station*, about a cabdriver. Those were the last things I wrote.

MG: Then there was a full stop.

HP: I didn't know where to go. I didn't know how to go anywhere. I couldn't continue to write plays about people who had been asleep for 29 years, although I'm sure a lot of other people have been asleep for 29 years. I felt obliged to investigate other territory, and I didn't know how to do it. That was true because my views were so strong about political issues, which I somehow felt I had to address. I didn't know how to do it because I can't write a play in which I know the end result. I've never done that. There's no play there if that's the case.

You know David Mamet said today in his interview that you can't write plays out of anger. I question that. Those three plays, *One for the Road*, *Mountain Language* and *Party Time*, were all written out of anger. I believe they don't suffer from that because it's a very cold anger. Icy. It's not anger which spills out all over the place. *Party Time* has never been done in the States. *Mountain Language* has hardly been done and *One for the Road* has hardly been done. And when it has been done, it has been done very badly. I was very upset by that. It was done disastrously in New York. The director was my old friend Alan Schneider, rest his soul, but it was a lousy production.

These plays, all of them, are to do not with ambiguities of power, but actual power. Now maybe this is not as appealing to some people as ambiguities of power, or shifting power, or how actual power is susceptible to all sorts of influences, psychological changes. But if I chose to write plays like *Mountain Language*, where you have the army and you have the victims, there's no ambiguity there. It is crude; that's the whole point. *Party Time* was to do with a hierarchy of power, which not only had it but was going to hang on to it, and actually use it, without any remorse or question whatsoever.

MG: Was that one of those rare parties you went to – *Party Time*?

HP: *Party Time* is not a documentary account of parties

I've actually been to or people I've actually met. It's the image that remains of the distinction between what happens upstairs at the party and what's going on down there in the street, and that's what interested me.

MG: To clarify, the period when you were not writing plays was after *A Kind of Alaska*.

HP: Yes. I'm sure that's absolutely right. This question of how many plays you write is ridiculous, how often you write a play, when's he going to write his next play. Quality doesn't depend on how often you do things.

MG: How do you measure the success of a play – your own feeling whether it works or not? Not the reviews?

HP: No, the thing itself.

MG: In terms of the writing, there's no appointment you have?

HP: [Pause.] No. And I feel fine about that. I need a bit of a break. But I certainly do not feel at a dead end.

MG: When is there going to be a change in the British government?

HP: I'm afraid I don't know the answer. To be realistic, I share with many other people a very strong sense of real depression about this country. The way out of it is to raise the consciousness of people. But I don't know how that is to be done. The first thing is to get rid of the present government.

MG: What about the monarchy? When will that end?

HP: Listen, I said I was interested in politics. I didn't say I was obsessed with it . . .

MG: Have you been to Buckingham Palace since your CBE?

HP: Two or three times. We were asked about two or three years ago to a very small State lunch for President Havel when he arrived here. There were only about a dozen or so people – mostly ambassadors, officials, diplomats, Antonia and me, a conductor who knew Czechoslovakia very well and a couple of others – and that was it. We all had to line up because he's the president. He didn't know I was going to be there. He had just arrived from Paris. The last time I saw him he was sprawling on his sofa in Prague having a number of drinks. He saw me and stopped and winked, and then we sat down at this table, and he leaned across the table and said, in the hearing of the Queen, 'Well, Harold, I never expected to find an unofficial playwright at lunch at Buckingham Palace.' He was, as you know, 'an unofficial playwright' for many years. But he was actually talking about me.

Afterword

Before leaving London, I visited the Pinter archives at the British Library. The magnificent high-vaulted Reading Room was filled with authors and scholars. A maze of corridors led to a large, cold storage space. Pinter occupies one section of the room with 60 boxes of material, arranged alphabetically. The *Moonlight* files begin with 19 pages of yellow-lined paper dating from 1978, followed by a scribbled notepad from Air Mauritius, an outline, drafts and completed manuscripts. Names of characters changed, as did words (codswallop was replaced by pigswill). Clearly, the play grew by a process of distillation.

The fact that the Pinter papers are enshrined in the British Library with the works of G.K. Chesterton and Evelyn Waugh should make him an immortal of English letters. But wait a minute! Look whose papers are in adjoining bookcases: the collected works of the Lord Chamberlain, for so many years the nation's official censor, arbiter of taste and gadfly to Pinter and other writers. Together with his staff of readers, he searched for improprieties and innuendo (dismissing *The Birthday Party* as 'an insane, pointless play' and *The Caretaker* as 'a piece of incoherence in the manner of Samuel Beckett'). He demanded excisions before licensing the plays to be seen by the public. This means that, in a final ironic coincidence, Pinter's manuscripts pass down to posterity in intimate proximity with the Lord Chamberlain's censorious reviews.

Acknowledgments

A number of people have been extremely helpful in the preparation and the writing of this book, beginning of course with Harold Pinter. Others include my wife Ann, my agent Owen Laster and Nick Hern. The first three conversations appeared in part in articles in the New York Times: 'A Conversation [Pause] With Harold Pinter,' 5 December 1971, in the New York Times Magazine; 'Harold Pinter: "I Started With Two People in a Pub",' 30 December 1979; 'Pinter's Plays Following Him out of Enigma and into Politics,' 6 December 1988.* The discussion at the 92nd Street Y in New York was organized by Karl Kirchwey, the head of that group's poetry series. The final four interviews took place over the course of a week in London in September 1993. Some of the material in those talks appeared in an article in *American Theatre*. My thanks to that magazine's editor, Jim O'Quinn, and to Pamela Kent at the New York Times London Bureau.

Index to Pinter's Work